HOMESPUN AND BLUE

A MODERN TREE OF LIFE BY THE AUTHOR

HOMESPUN AND BLUE

A Study of

American Crewel Embroidery

by

Martha Genung Stearns

BONANZA BOOKS

New York

Printed in the United States of America
Library of Congress Catalog Card Number 63-19875

This edition published by Bonanza Books,
a division of Crown Publishers Inc.,
by arrangement with Charles Scribner's Sons.

A   B   C   D   E   F   G

ACKNOWLEDGMENTS

AUTHOR	FIGURES 8, 12, 16, 18, 20, 22, 23, 24, 28, 29
CURRIER GALLERY OF ART, MANCHESTER, N. H.	FIGURES 15, 19
MRS. A. T. DUDLEY	FIGURE 21, PAGE 57
WILLIAM F. DUDLEY	FIGURE 31
MRS. FANNIE ELLIS	FIGURES 3, 14
MRS. BURTON GATES	FIGURE 17
MARY LAMPREY	FIGURES 6, 9
LONG ISLAND HISTORICAL SOCIETY,	
PHOTOGRAPH COURTESY OF BROOKLYN MUSEUM	FIGURE 1
METROPOLITAN MUSEUM OF ART	FIGURES 4, 7, 26, 27, 30
MUSEUM OF FINE ARTS, BOSTON	FIGURES 2, 5
NEW HAMPSHIRE HISTORICAL SOCIETY	FIGURES 10, 11
MRS. DANIEL O'HARA	FIGURE 25
MARGARET WHIPPLE, PHOTOGRAPH BY B. F. SWIEZYNSKI	FRONTISPIECE

FOREWORD

❋❋

This book, small though it is, is the result of years of searching and collecting in the field of early American needlework, and is intended to fill a gap. There are fine books on old bed quilts, whose designs have been named, copied and become classics. There are also books on samplers whose stiff little designs, many of them from pattern books, were made by children, and show their minds at work with small original touches, sometimes at a very early age, as they learned their letters and recorded things important to them. There are also many books of great historic value, richly illustrated, in which we find crewel work in the European manner.

But here we can study the individual freehand designs, drawn in most cases by the workers directly upon the fabric of woolens and linens probably from their own farms, and the threads spun and dyed by their own hands. These pieces are a most revealing expression of the worker's own thought, a very personal product of the women who had no small part in building the early homes of America. They are the record of the distaff side of the family.

Many people interested in needlework have studied in minute detail the collections in our museums and the great new collections where famous pieces have been photographed over and over. In order to tap a new vein, I went up and down through New England where very much creative work was done, visited local Historical Societies and borrowed from private owners. Many people have been most kind in lending their family treasures to a stranger for photographing. Now, twenty years later, some have died and their homes have changed hands or perhaps vanished altogether, so that all traces of these pieces have been lost. My hope is that this book may reveal to owners of such heirlooms what treasures they possess, in order that these may not be dispersed or destroyed.

In the illustrations which are the result, crude though some of the pieces are, one detects in the spirit of their makers' intense interest in life, observation of nature, and the recording of history as it reached them. A consecutive story is seen of the events which shaped the trend of their thought, and the simple arts of the people.

There is a saying that if you wait long enough, the old styles will come around again. In the case of handicrafts of the present day, this might seem very unlikely. This is an age of new inventions and every conceivable need is provided for with very little work of our own hands: new materials of synthetics and plastics which nature never knew; a great new range of colors has come into use, far from the soft vegetable dyes, and new designers produce designs and patterns by the thousand.

But the past history of our country remains the same, and in the first edition of this book I tried to show handwork that recorded it and pictured it in many cases at the time the events happened. The battle of Bunker Hill, the Boston Tea Party, the pine-tree shilling, and nature itself in a sparsely settled country where people lived by their own hard work were shown.

By some stroke of fate, crewel work has come back into favor and offers many possibilities for self-expression. The American style of this work lends itself to picturesque simplicity, more than does the elaborate, heavy, stitch-crowded style of the Jacobean period which could daunt the student. There is hope in this for a more interesting and spontaneous product. Perhaps we shall record, as a modern chapter of our history, the aeroplane, the submarine, skyscraper and moonscape. Who knows what lies ahead?

But I like to think that the impulse toward self-expression is not dead. Nature can play its part; the new interest in herbs, for instance, is already giving a basis for graceful and unusual designs, and in the herb garden lie some of nature's own colors.

Let us hope that there will always be some household use for beautiful handwork and creative thought, so that the generations coming may discern something of us as real, living people.

M. G. S.

Exeter, New Hampshire
1963

CONTENTS

✿✿

ILLUSTRATIONS

✿✿✿

[xi]

HOMESPUN AND BLUE

PASTURE ROCK

This is good New England rock,
Rooted in earth from which it grew,
And here the juniper berries lock
Blue with the giant-thistle blue.

This is solid New Hampshire stone—
Try to budge it and find you can't—
A hillside boulder bred to bone,
Starved on fire and fed on want.

Take in your flesh the granite groove,
Press it and let it leave its mark.
Hard and sweet on the hand as love,
This is sound rock born of dark.

FRANCES FROST

I

FRIENDLY WITH THE EARTH

❀❀❀

Ever since woman, the mother and home-maker, began to have a history, the needle has been her intimate companion. The singing kettle and the needle and thimble are inseparable parts of our picture of a home. Needle-decoration is an art, and as the art of a people is closely bound up with its daily life, needlework has been a medium, just as the pen and paint-brush have, for recording history.

If we think back to the years before there were daily papers and movies, sewing machines and department stores, even before there were roads, in America, we see women at work with their needles: making garments, mending and contriving, lovingly preparing for some family event, a birth or a marriage. They worked hard in those early homes, but much of their work became routine, almost subconscious, from habit, and did not confine their thoughts; indeed, there are few things so conducive to thinking as the small act of pushing a needle in and out. And when the materials with which they worked had been brought out of the very soil and prepared by those same hands, the result was bound to be something individual, recording some bit of the personality of that little family unit which in its turn had so vital a part in giving this country its first deep impress.

Their lives would seem to us unspeakably cramped and dull. There were few amusements or moments of recreation, little to read and few strangers to talk to. They had more time to think than we do in these feverish modern days, and they thought deeply about things—the meditation that goes with busy hands. National affairs and public events were considered from every angle and assumed deep importance. So it is that we find certain thoughts expressed in symbols and sewed into those early pieces of work which allow us to date them and to trace in some measure what was going on in America. There was their deep and somewhat fearful religious fervor; times of political excitement, when one showed one's preferences by putting a crown into a sampler, a Whig Rose on a coverlet, or, at the death of Washington, worked a weeping willow leaning over a tomb to join in expressing the national mourning. In 1785, a Frenchman and an American made the first balloon ascent from Calais, and every French snuff-box and trinket was decorated with a balloon to commemorate this conquering of the air by man; this "balloon furor" reached Boston a little later. Excitement comparable to this was the laying of the Atlantic cable, when a tangible link was established with the countries across the ocean. To a people who had been separated by thousands of miles of stormy gray water and weeks of precarious voyaging from the land of their forefathers, this cable shortened the distance in an almost miraculous manner, and we find the "endless chain" in stitches, and the cable pattern in rugs and glass and fabrics of that day. It is in such small ways that a national art is developed from the material of people's daily lives. Any one who studies American design in our handicrafts must study American history as well, for they proceed along parallel lines.

I remember a visit once paid to a New England country home, built in the third quarter of the seventeen hundreds. It was a fine old four-square house of perfect proportions, and the parlor was almost as it had been for a century. Everything in the room showed the work of women's hands: the sampler on the wall, the faded but beautiful handmade rugs, the polished lamp-chimneys and shining brasses, and cupboard full of carefully arranged old china. In a corner on a mahogany table stood a winter bouquet, silvery pods of "honesty" and feathery artemesia and a few tall stems of steel-blue globe thistle, arranged in a gray stoneware jar with a swirling bluebird painted into the glaze, its colors softly repeating the colors of nature in the hoarded sprays. As I studied it I could not help thinking, "Isn't that New England all over—the stone-gray and the blue!" That dried bouquet, the harvest of a past summer, was the final expression of the life going on in the dignified old room; the exquisite housekeeping which was responsible for the shining neatness everywhere, the absence of non-essentials, but leaving as an essential, beauty, expressed so clearly yet with restraint in the austerity of those subdued tones.

The gray-and-blue theme is repeated often in New England. It is common to the past and the present equally, because it grows out of nature. Those old stoneware jugs and jars with their blue birds and flowers and grapes are utterly familiar, made out of our soil. They remind us of sturdy old homespun to which time has imparted an ivory tone, embellished by our great-grandmothers with indigo threads, the blue softened by age and washings but still holding true. We who travel New England roads are always coming upon the same colors; a granite boulder in some upland meadow, with its shoulder sharp against a smoky-blue August sky; the deep indigo of mountains against the gray of November; a blossoming thistle in the angle of a stone wall, or the flash of a bluebird among gray branches in early spring. It is a product of the alchemy of air and sun and wind; it is in the very character of our stern and rock-bound ancestors, outwardly as hard as granite in their stern resolves, but blossoming into blue on their softer side, like a blue rift in a storm-cloud.

Those honest colors are restful, because of their basic strength; and when we find them illumined with rose and saffron and deep pine green, we have a subdued symphony of color as warm and glowing as country firelight. This is the theme which runs through the decorated fabrics wrought by our ancestors' hands which have come down to us, children of a very different age that we are. And it is the theme of this little book about New England needlework.

The life of those long-ago mothers was a struggle, for as the need for food, shelter and clothing will not wait, we see them always in a hurry, working against time—and nature will not be hurried. How little could they dream, those anxious housewives of long ago, that their life and the traces of their handiwork would be the subject of careful study two or three hundred years after, or that an Englishman visiting New England in 1933 would be writing:

It takes time to tame a countryside. Effort must cooperate with nature, nature with effort, if mankind is ever to seem, ever to be, at home in it. And many of these valley villages do indeed seem at home in their environment. The forced economy of level ground, the natural areas of clearance, the natural lines of watershed and rainfall, the use of local rock and wood in building, of water power in simple manufacture, have produced a modest seemliness that rises, at times, through interest to beauty. . . . Village carpentry bourgeons into as true a bit of style as you will find in America—the style of the New England cottage home, from the Connecticut valley to Provincetown and eastern Maine. Nor can you improvise that look of belonging to the ground these country homes take on. See how they stand friendly with the earth, which laps up to their sills like waves about a ship.*

We wish, as we see what their hands and nature and time working together have left for us, that they could know we love it and find it beautiful.

*America in Search of Culture: William Aylott Orton. Boston, Little, Brown & Co., 1933.

II

THE HISTORICAL BACKGROUND

✿✿

WE CAN cite no single event or place, nor any precise moment when it can be said "America began here." History is not a series of separate blocks which can be piled upon one another to build a structure. It is a great river, fed by countless smaller streams, perpetually in motion, with currents merging or coming in conflict, with an occasional great overflow, but always fluid, always flowing on. The Stream of Time is such a trite expression that one hesitates to use it; but it is none the less a true picture. America's beginning was an overflow from the parent stream which formed a new body, containing within itself something of all the flood of influences.

Christopher Dawson, writing about the Time-stream in his book *The Making of Europe*, says:

In prehistoric times Europe possessed no cultural unity. It was the meeting place of a number of different streams of culture which had their origin, for the most part, in the higher civilizations of the East, and were transmitted to the West by trade and colonization, or by a slow process of culture-contact. . . . The creation of a truly European civilization had its starting point in the Ægean, where there had arisen a centre of culture comparable to the higher civilization of Western Asia. And on the foundations of this development there finally arose the classical civilization of ancient Greece, which is the true source of the European tradition. It is from the Greeks that we derive all that is most

[5]

distinctive in Western as opposed to Oriental culture: our science and philosophy, our literature and art, our political thought and our conceptions of law. The defeat of Persia by the Greeks was really when the European ideal of liberty was born.

When we think, therefore, of the beginnings of American culture, we have to think back even before England, to the caravans from China and India, the market places of Alexandria and Cairo and Smyrna: to the network of Roman roads which spread all over Europe and the Near East from the gateways of Asia up to the coast of England, if we are to understand something of the currents which join in the River. History is still fluid, because it is by no means a complete record, nor ever can be. Not long ago, on the 2000th anniversary of Virgil's birth, the traces of a city were discovered on the coast of Albania. It was Butrinto, mentioned by Virgil in his story of the wanderings of Æneas as one of that hero's stopping places, but it had been thought to be legendary. Recent excavations have disclosed not only this, but a chain of other mighty cities along the transcontinental route to the East, which have been destroyed and forgotten. So the Barbarian invasions have wiped out whole populations and even the vestiges of their dwelling places; but they had their part in the scheme.

When America begins to appear in the commerce of nations and to tap this stream of culture for herself, we can imagine fantastic developments which may have a perfectly solid base in history but a conclusion which sounds like a fairy tale. We can picture some New England needlewoman on an outlying farm drawing her design and shaping its flowers and leaves and little animals, quite unconscious that she was indebted to many ancient peoples for its particular form; perhaps following some pattern laid down by the Chinese or Scythians and copied and carried from place to place by the little ships of Phœnicians or Greeks creeping along the great trade routes of the world. As G. K. Chesterton said,

"The modern progressives, who imagine that there is something new under the sun, are simply people who seriously underestimate the antiquity of the sun. Those who are most progressive do not really illustrate the idea of Progress, but rather the idea of Return."

To prove that this is not so fanciful as it may appear at first sight, we have the fact that Robert Adam, the Scottish architect whose work will be mentioned later on in the New England chronicle, visited the ruins of Diocletian's palace at Spalato in Dalmatia in 1757, and became so interested in its stately lines that he measured and sketched, surveyed and carefully restored its plan for his book of folio engravings which later became one of New England's architectural textbooks. There has always been some such adventurous Briton of inquiring mind who goes out more than half-way along the world stream and brings a cargo home with him.

The first colonists who came over to these northern shores came with a serious purpose. There are few races so closely bound to their homes and bits of land as the English, and it must have been a cause of the most solemn and urgent nature which could bring a company of people over the ocean in those days, when the journey was so hazardous and the future so unknown. Only their loyalty to a religious ideal, and a consuming desire for freedom to build homes in which they could be their own masters, could overcome their natural doubts and fears.

It was their bad luck to land on a difficult coast, with physical safety not secure. Great areas were heavily forested, or sandy, or steep and stony, inhabited by wild animals and by Indians who were an unpredictable element. From the very first, it was a struggle, and to meet it they had only the scanty supplies which their very moderate means had allowed them to bring. They were not well furnished to withstand the winter which was already at hand, and many of them died. Living conditions, in short, were necessarily those of peasants whose chief aim is to keep body and soul together.

[7]

But the Plymouth colonists were far from being peasants. They were the product of centuries of civilization and of long tradition, and they had a fair amount of education and much homely wisdom. Their aim from the first was to better themselves, and they brought well-developed minds and experience to it as well as the memory of better things, so that they were not content with rough, primitive ways. It was not long before the first hastily erected log cabins gave way to larger and better homes, and in a surprisingly short space of time they were beginning to accumulate possessions and live in comparative comfort.

The England upon which they had turned their backs in 1620 was the England of King James of the house of Stuart, and they landed upon a shore which had already been explored and mapped by Captain John Smith, who had named it New England. This band of pioneers has been celebrated in song and story, but perhaps nothing brings their plight home to us more clearly than the homely words of the "Forefathers' Song," which is attributed to one of their number and is to be found in the Massachusetts Historical Society's Collections. It was probably composed about 1630, and rings very true, dwelling upon the monotony of a diet of pumpkins and parsnips, and the depredations of birds and squirrels among the crops. One verse goes on:

> And now our garments begin to grow thin,
> And wool is much wanted to card and to spin.
> If we can get a garment to cover without,
> Our other in-garments are clout upon clout.
> Our clothes we brought with us are apt to be torn,
> They need to be clouted soon after they're worn,
> But clouting our garments they hinder us nothing;
> Clouts double are warmer than single whole clothing.

No draft animals nor sheep were brought on the *Mayflower's* first voyage and it was still some time before the breeding of domestic animals began. Wool, therefore, was scarce and precious, and when the garments they brought from home could be "clouted" no more, leather from the skins of wild animals and especially deerskin in the Indian style were called into service to make new ones. Surely needlework as an art was completely in abeyance in those days. But as Elder Brewster wrote during that first year, "It is not with us as with men whom small matters can discourage, or small discontentments cause to wish themselves at home again," and so in spite of the loss of half their original number and all sorts of privations, the intrepid band continued to hang on, as philosophically as they could, and thus the cornerstone of New England was laid.

In 1630 a substantial fleet of eleven ships under John Winthrop arrived to form the Massachusetts Bay colony, bringing many colonists and much gear, including cattle and sheep; and soon life might be said to be fairly under way. They were still working in a hurry—perhaps modern America comes naturally by its habit of "hustle"—but we reflect that America has had only three hundred years into which to crowd the growth and vast development of a nation which older countries took long ages and gradual slow changes to fulfill.

Over in the Dutch colony of New Amsterdam, which had been settled in 1614, things were very different. Not many miles away as the crow flies, it might have been a different world, for the Dutch housewives brought their comfortable habits with them; stores of household furnishings and linens, pillows and Delft and even silver, and the ample ways of ministering to hearty appetites to which they were accustomed.

In the southern colonies, too, life was much what it had been in England, and reached heights of actual elegance. There was no feeling of rancor against the mother country, and travel to and fro on business was common enough. Ladies went over to be presented at Court in rich costumes, and while perhaps not up to the latest minute in London fashions, they did themselves credit as Colonials of dignity and substance. Sons were sent to Oxford and Cambridge, and it all went to show that life in an English colony could be very smart and gay.

But the scene of our particular story lies in New England, and there the founding fathers kept their stern purpose always before the eyes of their flock, reminding them continually that the primary reason for their being here was a religious one. They seem to have had the Puritan inhibitions very strongly in Massachusetts Bay colony, and we picture them as wearing a perpetual frown. A slight laxity in dress brought forth a protest from the Massachusetts Court, forbidding the purchase of "any apparel, either woolen, silke or lynnen, with any lace on it, silver, gold, silk or threade. There shall be no cutt work, embroidered or needlework capps, bands or rayles . . ." This was the New England conscience in its early manifestation.

But as has often been pointed out, there were also Pilgrim Mothers; and women have their own ways of making life a little less rigid than an exclusively masculine regime would have it. The very fact that the English colonists brought their wives and children with them instead of coming in hunting parties like the French, or in military expeditions looking for gold and conquest like the Spaniards, meant that they wanted homes and domestic life to tie them to the soil; and these homes and the refining influence of women gradually opened out to embrace the whole community. "In our day," says Agnes Repplier, writing on the masterful Puritan, "it is generously conceded that the Puritans made admirable ancestors," but they could not have been comfortable people to live with. The women no doubt followed the line of least resistance where "cutt work and needlework capps" were concerned, but it would not have been in nature if they did not occasionally rebel.

It has been said that the households were run "under mother-and-daughter power," but every boy and man had an allotted share for his waking time. The heavy looms of those days were large and took up much floor space, but were an indispensable article of kitchen furniture, and almost every one knew how to weave, while spinning was second nature to them. The making of fabrics and clothing for the family was, of course, a feminine responsibility. They washed, carded, spun, wove, dyed, carrying the process through from the sowing of the flaxseed or the wool on the sheep's back, to the finished garment, at home. Every bit of cloth was precious, and it is no wonder that patch-work, the final end of any garments which had wear left in them, grew out of the early days. When wool began to be more plentiful, there was a formula for weaving a mixture most practical for hard wear, as follows: "One-third white wool, one-third black sheep's wool, one-third scraps dyed with indigo." This mixture resulted in a fabric which we know as Puritan gray; and gray, brown, and dull blue prevailed over all. "Sad-colored" clothing was the only wear. We can well imagine how hungry feminine nature grew for a little color and ease and release from these drab surroundings. To make a home in a wilderness, out of a rough cabin with no easy source of supply, took courage and resource, even in such self-reliant natures.

Nearly every one grew flax; in the Connecticut colony in 1640, it was ordered by the General Court that "every family within these plantations shall procure and plant this present year at lest one spoonfull of English hempe seed in fruitful soyle at leaste a foot distant betwixt each seed." Those fields of intensely blue blossoms must have been a delight to the eyes, of which even the civic authorities could not deprive them. When the flax had gone to seed, the stalks were carefully pulled and stacked until dry, and the seed threshed out for future planting. Then the stalks, of a rough, stringy fiber, were soaked in water for two or three weeks and spread on the grass to be rotted. When the soft parts had sufficiently rotted away, a long process of hatchelling and pounding and combing and bleaching began. The action of water and sun played a great part; and after the thread was woven into long strips of many yards, it was laid out on the grass and subjected to further alternate wettings and dryings. The result of this labor and natural purifying process was linen of rough, iron-wearing quality, which grew only whiter and softer with hard usage.

Sheep, which in 1644 were estimated at only about 3000, began to multiply under rigorous protection. They were treated like pets, allowed to graze at will, and never used for food during those early years. Every scrap of wool was used, even the yellowed "tag-locks" which went with the other odds and ends into the dye-pot. This pure-wool fabric did not differ very much from the weaving of Bible times, or of primitive peoples, for the process is exactly the same. There is no craft, with the exception of the handling of clay on the potter's wheel, which has changed so little with the passage of many centuries. So Nature entered intimately into the textiles from the past, in the growing of flax and the long stages through which it passes into thread; the spongy texture of the wool soaking up and retaining the colors yielded from common plants through simple processes; and finally, the human use and wear and the washings and dryings. There is something elemental about it all—the way man was meant to live, in direct cooperation with nature.

The Puritan housewife had to be proficient in amateur chemistry as well as many other arts and sciences. What searching and experimenting must have gone on with boiled roots and barks, plant and berry juices, in the hunt for dyes and fixatives. Did she recognize the wayside weeds of her new country, and know the properties of hickory and butternut, sumac and birch and cherry? Indigo was always to be relied upon because it was fast, and strong enough to be used in any degree of intensity, covering up small discolorations. This was doubtless the reason for the prevalence of "blue and white" in the early textiles and their decoration, though the native New England "false indigo," or baptesia, yielded only a poor quality and a better had to be got from the South. She must test the powers of the golden lichens which clung to New England rocks, and the bright wild flowers, perhaps learning something of Indian lore to fill in her chromatic scale. The greens were elusive, because they had to be made with yellows blended with indigo; threads from different "boilings" would come out in varying shades, giving the early work its delightful vagaries in color, blues and greens merging together as in the soft harmonies of Oriental rugs. Browns and yellows were the very colors of nature and plentiful enough. Red was the one color lacking in the early color-scale; madder gave only a muddy tint, and pokeberry juice had an underdepth of purple, and it was not until cochineal was introduced that the range of pinks and reds was filled up with reliable shades.

With all the manifold tasks of such households on their hands, we wonder just when it was that women had time for any thought of decorating the textiles they created. Little is known about the needlework of the first half-hundred years, except for mentions of embroidered pieces in old inventories and wills. How fascinating it would be to study a piece of work from America's childhood! By reason of strength alone, many pieces should have survived, for they were sturdy enough. But, partly because they were worn out in one form of hand-me-down or another, and partly because succeeding generations did not recognize their value and have discarded or destroyed them, we can only speculate, and still search hopefully through old trunks and chests on the chance that something may still be lying overlooked and unrecognized.

Two, and perhaps three, samplers crossed the Atlantic with the Plymouth colonists. But samplers are a whole subject in themselves, calling for a special technique, and their designs were seldom original with the worker. The subject has been so admirably covered in other books that we shall not dwell on it here, save to point out that the early colonists were skillful with the needle, and brought over with them, either in actual stitches or in living memory, designs which were identical with those popular in England in that day, to provide inspiration for American workers to follow. The chief difference in this transplanted art is that because of the lack of trained skill in designing and limitations in the choice of materials it became simplified; but if it lost in detail and intricacy, it gained in strength and vigor. We have another element to reckon with in the Puritan's distaste for decoration or display, which was waiting to stifle any form of artistic exuberance at its birth. So let us think of the first work of the colonist women in its delayed flowering, as bold and simple, done on strong fabrics in few colors with blue mightily predominant, in the stitches which they could remember or easily invent, and expressing their own strong personalities in the design. We know very well what England was producing in the seventeenth century, and it may be illuminating to spend a little time in considering what must have been entirely familiar to the eyes of the English-born settlers of this country.

Many diverse influences were at work which made the artistic expression of that period extremely complicated and elaborate. The heavy Tudor style, though passing, was still in evidence. Just as Tudor furniture of massive oak is heavy, with great bulbous legs and bold carving, the embroidered scrolls and plant forms were large and bold in outline; their resemblance to the natural flower and leaf was obscured by tortured twistings and scallopings, and a multiplicity of stitches added to the appearance of unrest. The needleworkers who decorated these textiles seemed to feel that they must follow the idea of a woven fabric in which the pattern runs all the way through, and did their best to cover the whole area with stitchery. Perhaps this was due to an unconscious clinging to the concept of pictured tapestries. Tent-stitch and appliqué vied with each other in covering the groundwork, and trees and vines in heavy growth branched out in all directions. Even when various fauna and heraldic devices were introduced, they were surrounded by all manner of fruits and flowers and foliage.

At the end of Elizabeth's reign the formation of the East India Company had brought a direct Oriental influence into England, which artists had incorporated into their designs. Versions of the Tree of Life, of tropical plants and flowers, and birds with brilliant plumage began to show themselves among the English oaks and roses. The pomegranate and pineapple grew absurdly from the same stem as the foxglove and the honeysuckle. When the potato and the strawberry were introduced into English agriculture, the blossom of the one and the red fruit of the other figured often in the foregrounds, welcomed for their novelty and interest; peacocks, parrots, and birds of Paradise taken from the Indian textiles disported themselves among the branches, giving great scope for color.

As the centuries brought the tide of travel and commerce up across Europe, many accumulations were added from every country through which it passed. England during the Tudor and Stuart times was in the full flood of these mingled currents, and if we were to attempt to analyze them all, this account would soon pass beyond manageable limits. It is possible to name only a few of the stronger influences and give some typical examples. It is very plain to see that the floral subjects which are the direct ancestors of American embroideries grew from seeds sown in the East.

China, India, and Persia each contributed largely to the work, and may be briefly characterized as follows. From India's ancient art comes the idea of growth from the soil, of trees and large floral forms rooted in a series of little hillocks worked in the earth colors, browns and greens. The characteristic Tree of Life is the symbol of the life principle itself;

the leaves and other forms which grew upon its branches often contained within their outline an inner flower or subordinated spray, symbolizing the seed containing the potential tree or the blossoming plant entire. This tree in Christian symbolism came to mean the tree which grew in Paradise, and as the cross is spoken of as a Tree, it became linked with the thought of man's redemption as well as with his fall. Indian design as a whole is symmetrical and full of alternations.

Persian design is also rich in floral forms, more frank and natural than the Indian, and gaining in grace and freedom; while Chinese floral design combines in an interesting degree both ideas; for whereas the peonies and chrysanthemums and fruit blossoms are pictured in a completely naturalistic manner, giving a first impression of freedom, it is found upon holding up a length of the woven textile or other fabric that they are strictly confined within unseen lines, and have all the rhythm of repetition. The Chinese motives are rich in symbolism. One development of this which occurs over and over again is the suggestion that every good gift comes to man from the sea, so that the trees and flowers often grow out of a conventional wave-form, with motion in its undulating line. Nothing in these Oriental growths ever ends vaguely in a broken stem or a loosely trailing line, but springs from a fold of earth, a wave, a scroll, or grows from a vase in the Persian manner.

India was probably the first country to bring the art of dyeing to its highest development; but in the fourteenth century Italy was beginning to usurp the mastery. Florence was the chief city in Europe for the dyer's trade, and magnificent silk brocades and other rich fabrics were woven in Italy, until the looms of Lyons in France rose to fame as rivals. An example of what happened in the slow migration of art is afforded by the little motive called the Florentine "artichoke." It came by way of India, Persia, and Sicily to the Italian looms by reason of its regular shape and symmetry which made it a good weaving pattern, as well as its ornamental value. Its ranks of overlapping leaves bear a relationship also to the growth of the Chinese lotus flower. England's merchant marine brought these fabrics to decorate the wealthy homes of England, and from these imported textiles it was natural enough for the English needleworkers to copy the form in their silk and wool stitchery. Much later, in the eighteenth century, we find this little artichoke form appearing in American crewels, but having lost its Eastern origin, for it is described in a book on early American design as the houseleek, or "hen-and-chickens," familiar in country dooryards. This is but one instance among many of our workers making the exotics their own.

Since the world was created records have been kept by means of pictures, and among all the many methods of representing figures and events, embroidery has an important place, the needle ranking with the pen, the brush, and the chisel. One art has given place for a time to another in turn; but all through the past the Christian faith inspired its devotees to express their zeal and love by creating beauty for the service of the Church. It was the Church in the Middle Ages which was the greatest patron of art, and patient hands with the needle and the illuminator's brush have given us an unequalled record of the growth and influence of Christianity. And within the actual forms depicted, there lay the second meanings, the underlying mysterious language of symbolism. During the centuries before the printed word was common, the people had grown skilled in reading this language of symbols, which we can still see in the cathedrals and domestic architecture of Europe. Every flower, every color, every animal, both real and mythical, had some attribute which lent it a scriptural or historical meaning, and stories were told in carved wood and stained glass. The Bible itself is full of symbolism, and of teachings under the guise of parables, and both the Old and the New Testaments lay open to the unlettered by means of pictures. Every incident had its recognized expression: Noah and the

Ark, which represented the Church rising triumphant above the flood; Jonah and the whale, which was a prefiguring of the Resurrection; the apple which represented the fall of man, the fish which meant his baptism, the palm of martyrdom, the trefoil of the Trinity, and countless others. The simple people of those days were just as quick to recognize Saint Peter by his keys, Saint Sebastian by his arrows, and King Louis of France by the fleur-de-lys, as we should be in reading their names.

The royal arms of England and the European countries and the badges of princely houses were a riot of animals, flowers, and all sorts of conventionalized objects, multiplied by quarterings; and knights wore heraldic devices on armor, dress, and banner. But heraldry had grown out of the earlier Christian symbolism which formed a whole picture-language; and a knowledge of this fully systematized picture-language opens up a new world of meanings in design. London was one of the world's great centers as an important market place, as well as the seat of the English Court, and anything which found favor at Court at once became the fashion. Needlework had been very much the fashion for a long time, for it was practised by many royal ladies, even back to Anglo-Saxon times. Catherine of Aragon introduced the Spanish style of embroidery on fine linen. Elizabeth was a skilled needlewoman, and encouraged by her love of lavish dress the elaboration of the art. The peacock and the swan were royal birds, as the lion was the king of beasts, and roses, thistles, and lilies were everywhere.

Besides the animals of the natural kingdom, there were a host of mythical ones which had been introduced during the Middle Ages by the quaint old Bestiaries, or "Beast-books." These can best be described as travellers' tales, which lost nothing in the telling, for the benefit of the credulous who stayed at home. A great portion of the globe was still unexplored when these books were popular, and those travellers who ventured along the fringe of the unknown, and sailors who had been shipwrecked on strange islands, came home with tales of mermaids, dragons, unicorns, of the phœnix which though destroyed by fire rises again from its ashes, of tritons, nereides, and sea elephants. From Homer, who speculated about the unknown sea lying beyond his ken, down to Sir Walter Raleigh, who brought tobacco to England and whose men told terrifying tales to simple villagers of having seen savages blowing out smoke from their nostrils, there were signs and wonders which engaged the fancy of the needleworkers and could be wrought upon the fabric they had in hand. Simple people are slow to change, and they loved such tales and handed them down by word of mouth.

With the romantic and melancholy fortunes of the Stuart family, England entered upon a time of political activities and intrigues, religious animosities, and violent partisanships. The Stuart era as regards our art runs from 1603, when the reign of James I began, through that of Queen Anne, daughter of James II, who came to the throne in 1702 and died in 1714. We are told that this lady was a skillful needlewoman herself, and certainly a great improvement in design and many graceful works are characterized by her name. It is strange to turn from a contemplation of this gentle employment to the fact that a long and bloody struggle with the French and Indians in America was called Queen Anne's War, lasting for twelve years, the Deerfield massacre in the Connecticut valley taking place in 1704.

Now we must look among all the riotous floral growth for all sorts of hidden meanings, symbols, devices, and ciphers, in which a miniature history of those devious times can be read. Mary Queen of Scots spent her years of captivity with a needle in hand, and her letters to friends are full of requests for fine thread from abroad. In a letter of that time she is quoted as saying that "all day she wrought with hir Nydill, and that the Diversitie of the Colors made the Worke seme less tedious." How many women of all times could say the same! Professor Francis de

Zulueta, in his careful and minute study of the embroidered hangings at Oxburghe Hall in Norfolk, several of which were made by the Queen, makes us conscious of their value as a true historical document in a whole series of pictorial symbols. Mary must have foreseen her approaching tragic end, for she worked her own arms with a device of a hand with a knife cutting down a vine, with the motto: Virescit Vulnere Virtus (Virtue flourisheth by a Wound). And in another place she made an oak tree surrounded by the legend, Integrity is more lasting than Oak. The acorn was a Stuart emblem, and the caterpillar also, perhaps because the "canker" among the flowers depicted the treason at work against the Queen. This is only one example of the needle's activity in those years; it has left an extraordinarily rich legacy behind. Add to all these influences the vast variety of stitches, the ingenuity displayed in all manner of fillings for leaf and flower petal, and you have a whole of such elaboration that the eye has nowhere to rest. The final extravagance of the Stuart style was the "stump work," which developed the stuffing of the figures into raised forms and the appliqué of separate material to such an extent that needlework was debased to absurdities like little dolls fastened to a background of fabric. This particular style so far as we know never reached America.

The principal stitches used on the monumental Jacobean pieces were: outline, rope, cable, chain, coral, and couching stitches for the stems and bold outlines. Satin stitch, long and short shading stitch and blocks of laid stitches suggesting the diapered backgrounds painted in illuminated manuscripts, filled in the forms; a whole spray might be worked within the outline of a leaf, flowers within flowers, and dark contrasting with light. We cannot indicate in short space the infinite variety of the Jacobean needlework.

The style characterized by Queen Anne's name gained not only in sanity but in lightness and grace. Workers lost their fear of leaving areas uncovered and began to space their designs by breaking them up into separate plants and flower sprays. Borders became more important, and sometimes a central medallion was introduced with a monogram or device, and scattered small figures surrounded it.

A room in an English home then might look rather austere to us, its furniture being spare though important and massive. Tables were covered with a cloth of some kind, which was called a "carpet" to distinguish it from the "tapet" on the floor. These table-carpets were very often of Turkey-work, or a copy of the Turkish rugs made with the Ghiordes knot of which we shall speak later. Beds were important pieces of furniture and of great size, and needlework was lavished upon furnishings for them. The chilly English winters and unheated bedrooms called for as much shelter from drafts as possible, either actual or by suggestion, and curtains and valances were made as well as coverlets to shroud the bed's occupant as if he were in a tent. Large hangings on the walls and heavy curtains at the windows doubtless were for the same purpose. The bed-hangings as well as the beds themselves were valued possessions very often mentioned in old inventories and wills, from which we may learn the details of long-vanished splendors. For instance, there is the bed inherited by King Richard II from his mother, "of red velvet, embroidered with ostrich feathers in silver, and heads of leopards in gold, with boughs and leaves issuing out of their mouths," and much later there is a record of "a bed of gold swans with branches and flowers of divers colors."

These wall-hangings, chair-seats, and bed-furnishings of the Jacobean period, with which every needlewoman of today is familiar, give us an idea of what probably formed the ideal of a well-furnished home to the minds of the American colonists. When they tried to translate these things into American, with hands unaccustomed to designing, we can picture something of the result. It would be strange if a little bit of "wishful thinking" and homesickness were not sewed into the work. But as for all the political symbolism rampant in the home country during the Stuart times, we can well believe that much was lost in transit.

Marcus B. Huish says:

Tapestry pictures have such a Royalist air about them that it is hardly probable that they found favour with the Puritan damsels of the Stuart reigns, and consequently, it may be doubted whether the fashion for making them crossed the Atlantic to the New World with the Pilgrim Fathers, or those who followed in their train. Samplers, on the other hand, with their moralities and their seriousness, would seem to be quite akin to the old-fashioned homes of the New Englanders, and doubtless there must be many specimens hanging in the houses of New England and elsewhere which were produced from designs brought from the Old Country, but over which a breath of native art has passed which imparts to them a distinctive interest and value.*

Every one interested in early needlework is doubtless familiar with Lora Standish's sampler which hangs in Plymouth Hall, and with that of Anne Gower, the first wife of Governor Endicott, which is now in the Essex Institute, Salem. The oak and the rose are much in evidence. But it was inevitable that for the rank and file of sampler-makers to follow, the oak should be an American oak, and the rose, instead of the badge of the Tudors, should be from their own garden; the strawberries and squirrels and birds and deer were those to be seen from their own door. The political significances and *doubles-entendres* were probably soon lost, and only the forms remained.

King James I was interested, in 1620, to establish a factory in England for needlework pictures, where Flemish workmen made with the needle an imitation of a woven tapestry, and used as their subjects scenes from the Bible, and Pagan gods and heroes from the classics. Under the royal patronage these became all the rage, and are what Mr. Huish refers to as "tapestry pictures." But our colonists about this time were far too

Samplers and Embroideries: by Marcus B. Huish. Longmans, Green & Co., 1913.

preoccupied to sit down to this sort of elegant employment, and pictures contributed little to the native art, for pieces for which the designs may be bought ready for working and carried out by another hand lose interest because they show no originality and become too plentiful.

One feels a little differently about the "pattern books" full of small designs of flowers, birds, beasts, and fish, because they give the worker a great range to choose from, and she may arrange and change the details to suit herself. By means of these pattern books all sorts of designs and motives circulated through Europe. They were especially numerous in German but were copied and translated into other languages, added to, and changed until their authorship in the beginning is almost impossible to trace. Many early ones give designs on squared lines which could be followed not only by workers in cross-stitch but by weavers and lace-makers; others have designs which have been later identified in jewelry and goldsmith work, inlay, even architectural detail. We find little borders which may be run across in museum collections in the variously decorated fabrics from Italy, Spain, Portugal, France, and the Low Countries, so wide a circulation did these little handbooks attain. The English editions of some of these compilations have such titles as "A Scholehouse for the Needle" and "The Needle's Excellency." Mrs. Luke Vincent Lockwood, writing in the bulletin of the Needle and Bobbin Club, speaks of a book of small designs of the late sixteenth century containing 124 birds and 16 sorts of four-footed beasts and 52 fish, which would give the worker a good deal of scope. She adds:

These small designs lent themselves well to smaller objects, such as cushions and cupboard cloths, and though I do not know of a single example of this work done before 1700 surviving here, there can be no doubt that it was done by colonial women in great quantities. A Salem, Mass. inventory dated 1647 enumerates 'a parcel of cruell thread and silk,' and another dated 1654, 'cruell and fringe.' In Salem, Mass., also, in 1672, 'a small box with severall samplers, laces and Broidered works.' These are all references to materials for needlework. The fact that it was done in wool has something to do with its disappearance, and the few surviving examples of turkey work have escaped the moths by a miracle, for they are the most tempting morsels.

The bed-cover illustrated in Fig. 15, although probably much later in date, shows signs of having been influenced by a pattern book, for the worker has methodically arranged all the fruit trees in a row: apple, peach, pear, plum and cherry, and has also introduced the berries—grape, currant, barberry, strawberry, and so on; these designs are better drawn than the rest of the plan, which is obviously her own, or if not by a less-trained hand.

The earliest actual pieces which we have from those first seventy-five years of America, aside from samplers, are specimens of Turkey work, which was inspired in England by the importation of rugs from the Near East. These were finding their way into many English and European homes, and are to be seen in paintings of that period. Vermeer paints them with minute care in his Dutch interiors, and Hans Holbein introduces some into his portraits, notably the one of Georg Gisze. In this country we have an example or two in John Singleton Copley's portraits. This style of needlework in rug-knots on a coarse linen ground called for a complete covering of the basic fabric with stitches, another example of the all-over tendency ingrained from the long acquaintance with tapestries, where color and design make the whole piece into a single subject. This work became popular in America, for the heavy fabrics and threads lent themselves well to this style and it was easy to do. There is an example of early Turkey work surviving in the Essex Institute, and many mentions of it in old records. We are having a revival of it today, in logical succession to the Jacobean and petit-point styles which have recently been so popular.

But again, there was not much originality in this type of angular design so obviously taken direct from Oriental sources and adapted from a sister art. We are more interested in trying to trace some distinctive contribution to the art of needlework design made by the colonial women themselves, some small creation of mind and hand which will give us an insight into their thought. Let us turn again for a moment, therefore, to consider the progress of historical events on this side of the Atlantic.

III

COLONIAL NEW ENGLAND

❀❀

In 1636, only sixteen years after the *Mayflower's* historic voyage, Harvard College was founded, and young men from different parts of New England gathered there in their imported broadcloths or country homespuns, according to their circumstances. The year 1639, incidentally, saw the introduction of the printing press, and this was to have its influence in the dissemination of all sorts of information and the forming of public opinion. Life was more comfortable, although money was short; it was necessary to send cash payments to England for needed commodities, and somehow the coins never came back. Payment in kind, barter and exchange was the rule. There was an early coin, minted in England for the use of the colonies, called the Rosa Americana, because it carried the Rose of the royal badge, a five-petalled open flower which survives under many names and guises in American designs. We shall see it later on the stamps which started all the trouble over the Stamp Act in 1765. But even when it became the Rose of Sharon and the Whig Rose of the later patchwork bedquilts, or the top-heavy blossoms on little girls' samplers, it bears a strong family resemblance to the rose which Queen Mary Tudor embroidered on the cover of her prayerbook, and the carved stone roses which alternate with the Tudor portcullis among the arches of King's College chapel in Cambridge,

England, where so many of New England's early divines were educated. Truly this was a transplanted flower which made a strong growth and held its type for generations; the conventionalized heraldic form was not softened into a more naturalistic semblance for many years.

In 1652 the Massachusetts Legislature set up a mint, and the first coins struck in this country bore the Pine Tree. An early New England silversmith named John Hull, who was born in England in 1624, left this statement in his diary, recorded in 1652:

Upon occasion of much counterfeit coin brought into this country, and much loss accruing in that respect . . . the General Court ordered a mint to be set up, and to coin it. . . . And they made choice of me for that employment: and I chose Robert Sanderson to be my partner, to which the Court consented.

The best known of their coins was the pine-tree shilling, a thin little silver coin unevenly stamped; there is a story that when John Hull's daughter was married, he gave her for a marriage portion her own weight in pine-tree shillings, which would come to a very substantial sum. The little pine-tree motive appears so often in green crewel wool on bed-testers and in stiff angular lines on samplers and other worked pieces that we cannot help tracing a relationship, despite the several different mediums, to New England's great pines, growth of her virgin forests, which were so much in demand for tall masts for the King's ships. The finest were marked for cutting by the broad arrow which designated the property of the crown, and there is a record in Rockingham County, N. H., to this day of a pine tree bearing the arrow which was 111 feet tall and 8 feet in diameter at the butt. Perhaps some little girl in the neighborhood of Newmarket recorded the fall of this giant with her needle. There were several small episodes in early village histories of difficulties placed in the way of the King's surveyors endeavoring to carry out their duty and collect the finest trees—episodes which might have brought on an outbreak similar to the Boston tea-party if New Hampshire people had been more inflammable. Later, in 1700, the Massachusetts Colony rallied to a flag which bore a pine tree on a white field, and the first war vessels commissioned by Washington flew the pine tree at the top of American masts, a significant reversal in American fortunes.

What is there more English than the oak, its leaves and its acorns? These forms are very numerous on samplers dated between 1648 and 1700, reduced to the angles necessary in cross-stitch and Holbein stitch. We have seen the oak's close connection with the Stuart family, and it took on additional significance after the flight of Charles II, who was sheltered by an oak. The motive was universal in England, and put into strictly conventional form it appears in the early American pieces. In more freehand style it continues to grow in the crewel embroideries, springing from stems and waving its scalloped leaves along borders. Could not this characteristic design have merged into the later patriotic one of the Charter Oak, at the time of the Charter episode in Connecticut when that precious document was hidden in a great oak tree to keep it from being surrendered to Sir Edmund Andros the Viceroy, in 1687?

There is still another tree which frequently occurs in natural form and growth. The New England primer says, "In Adam's fall we sinnéd all," and the apple tree, with or without Adam and Eve, has a true New England flavor, with its bright fruit of mammoth size, and is very popular with the needleworkers.

Another design which was used often in different ways on both sides of the Atlantic was the Prince's Feather. This appears over and over on coverlets and other domestic articles, and its original is one of the three curved plumes of the Prince of Wales's crest. It is picked out in gold on the heraldic shields adorning the tomb of the Black Prince who first assumed it, in Canterbury Cathedral, and it was the chosen device of his son King Richard II. There is a coverlet worked entirely in fine yellow chain-stitch in the Victoria and Albert Museum showing this graceful plume design, which became very popular afterward as a quilting pattern in America. Loyalty to the reigning house first inspired its use, but its decorative form made it a popular design long after its significance had been forgotten, so that it even survived the purge of the Revolution. It sometimes was almost indistinguishable from the long, fern-like leaves which were common in crewel embroidery.

A little running stag is often seen in crewel borders, and this is a motive with a long history. In religious symbolism, it pictures the soul flying from the powers of evil, which are usually represented by hounds; it also reminds us of the Biblical reference to the "hart panting for the water brooks," or the soul longing for the water of eternal life. Straight down through the centuries it comes, accumulating history and legend, and at one time it was a national emblem of England. The deer on the crown lands were dedicated to the royal chase and were protected from other hunters and poachers. Innumerable references in Shakespeare's plays and in such popular favorites as the story of Robin Hood in Sherwood Forest will come to mind, showing how it is bound up with literature as well as history. Perhaps the running stag as a needlework pattern crossed the ocean in living memory, as well as in little pattern books, but New England's own forests were full of deer which played an important part in the domestic economy.

From Eastern sources there is the carnation, reaching us by way of England from India and Persia. This flower with its fringed petals spreading out fanwise from their sheath is omnipresent in Persian ornament, and as a weaving pattern on European looms; and as no American garden was complete without its spicy fragrance, the crewel designs have made the most of it, though sometimes its original contours become confused through freehand drawing. It is often associated with another Persian idea, discernible in the vase or jar from which flower and tree shapes spring. This seems to trace back to the movable gardens in pots which are so common in hot countries where the long dry season bakes the soil to powder. An Eastern garden takes on the nature of an oasis, where water and shade are quite as important as flowers, and blossoming plants and shrubs are moved about as the life of the family shifts between roof and courtyard and cool interior.

The tulip, which probably reached America first with the Dutch settlers, had long been blossoming in the floral medley on the embroidered Tree of Life, and also appears in the decoration of silver by John Hull, he of the pine tree shilling. This flower, a little chalice held erect on a straight stem rising from graceful curved leaves, has the clean lines beloved of artists of all times. It is a much travelled design, for we find it in almost every country; it lent itself especially well to the woven brocades of Italy because of its symmetrical shape, which, even when strictly confined so as to reverse on the loom, was still graceful and natural.

Something happened about this time which gave the weaving industry a lift and therefore lightened the housewives' burden, as well as helping to improve the quality of American textiles. Twenty families of weavers from Yorkshire came over and settled in Rowley, Mass., bringing the parts of a fulling mill with them, which was set up in 1634. This group of expert craftsmen gradually percolated through New England, particularly New Hampshire; several families settled in Londonderry and from thence subdivided among other small towns. They sowed the seed of the weaving industry broadcast, and from this time on, Governor Winthrop speaks of homespun industries as general, though "Rowley exceeded all the towns." What is more, these trained craftsmen handed down their art to their children, for in several cases there were noted weavers in these localities generations afterward.

By the middle of the seventeenth century, the colonies had grown so much in wealth and self-reliance that England began to be alarmed, as her trade showed signs of falling off. A writer of that period says that "all the wigwams, huts and hovels the English dwelt in at their first coming" had given way to comfortable and even spacious houses which had sprung up all over southern New England, and this is amply confirmed by those which are still standing in dignified old age. The Wayside Inn at Sudbury, for example, was built in 1686.

For years before this the Indians had been telling tall stories of the great river which ran north and south through rich hunting and trapping country, with virgin forests of great trees. The rivalry between the Dutch and the English over the settling of this new tract had been decided in favor of the English because of their superior numbers and their natural inclination for exploring. From the settlements at Hartford and Wethersfield, men had pushed up the Connecticut River to Springfield, and now settlers went through unbroken forest inland from Massachusetts Bay, by what is still known through the Mount Holyoke country as the Bay Path; and a string of villages followed the rich river meadows. The furthest one in 1669 was Westfield, due west from Boston. In the same way New Hampshire people had worked in along the Piscataqua River and founded very early the towns of Hampton, Exeter, Durham, Dover, and a string of fishing and shipping villages clustered around the Kennebec. These isolated handfuls of English home-makers centered their log houses around log forts and encircled them with stout stockades, doing their farming with a gun always handy.

The cruel French and Indian wars which ravaged the country in Queen Anne's reign left the names of martyr-villages written in blood— Hadley, Hatfield, Sunderland. The massacre of Deerfield, Massachusetts, by a force of French and Indians coming down from the Canadian border was to come in 1704, but depredations by the Indians had begun in 1675 with the terrible Bloody Brook massacre, still called in Deerfield the "fight in the meadow," or "at the bars," as if it still lived in memory. These outbreaks multiplied until King Philip's War flared up in earnest. The cause of the enmity was partly due to misdeeds on both sides, but there might not have been open war if the French had not stirred up some hostile Indian tribes to take part in their quarrel with the English.

Outbreaks were to be feared almost anywhere, and Berard says: "For years no isolated band of settlers felt secure by night or day, and many a happy home and thriving village fell a prey to the savages, while these cruel wars lasted." Many of the records of those fearful days bear unmistakable signs of having come down from actual participants, handed down as household tales from grandfathers to wide-eyed children, with all the homely details which give them reality. The bank of a pond or the angle of a fence would be the scene, and "it was on a Sunday, in very hot weather." From Durham comes the tale, "In ye dead of ye night, there were doors knocked at and stones flung," by Indians seeking to know how many houses were empty. Durham was decimated, its houses burned, and many women and children "captivated," in July, 1694. Such memories were burned into the minds and hearts of the survivors never to be forgotten while they lived. But we are shown the silver spoons which Great-grandmother triumphantly rescued by hiding them in her capacious pocket as she ran.

In 1692, the two colonies of Plymouth and Massachusetts Bay were united under the name of Massachusetts, giving us again a suggestion of the native blue, for the name is said to be taken from an Indian word meaning "blue hills." At this point in the history of the New England colonies, we find them a homogeneous group of English descent. New York and New Jersey had been settled by the Dutch, Delaware by the Swedes, Pennsylvania had a large percentage of Germans, and the Carolinas were very much under French influence. Many new national strains and influences were shortly to enter New England, and difficult days were ahead; but this particular time makes a momentary stopping place, for it is the end of "early American history." The founders were dead, and with them died the last personal memories and contacts with their faraway birthplace. Their sons and grandsons, born on American soil, were now to carry on.

THE GOLDEN AGE

❋❋❋

Now the world came pouring into New England through its gateway towns. The territory now divided into the six New England states had been encompassed by sea, and important towns had naturally developed along its best harbors. American merchants and captains were beginning to build their handsome houses in Portsmouth, Salem, Newport, and to fill them with rich furnishings from many foreign lands.

National affairs and events large with political significance are recorded on the pages of history for future generations to ponder over, when the results of early trends can be traced and judged. But there is another kind of record, a homespun history, which is handed down from father to son, from mother to daughter, made up of small domestic events, far nearer to its people. It plays a vital part in shaping the characters who shape a country's history. A straw, slight and valueless in itself, may yet show which way the wind blows, and perhaps a needle and thread can tell us much of the mind of the woman who wields it. America in its homespun period was built of family units, who gained their living and perhaps amassed wealth by their own labor and resource, accustomed to think and act for themselves. They had not yet been drawn into the mass formation which characterizes our own day. We are rich in records, both written and pictured in various forms of art, of the years from 1700 to

1775, during which America reached its peak in native architecture and handicrafts, and perhaps in dignified living.

From now on, we have newspapers, with quaint spelling and type sinking deeply into the rag paper. *The Boston Gazette* was founded in 1704. Domestic chronicles reach us, too, from old letters and diaries and account books. It was the day of the copied letter, especially in business houses, where this was the laborious method of keeping records of trans-actions, along with the columns of figures on the tall pages of old ledgers. From such a homely source we know today that a lady of Concord, New Hampshire, who must have been a model of virtue and industry from her mother's knee to attain such proficiency, spun 210¾ runs of yarn in ten months, at the age of seventy-one. Every country community had its master craftsman and prodigy of endurance and skill, and they are set forth in the old town histories, not to mention the details inscribed on their ancient tombstones.

To recapitulate: we have as a small capital for the future American needlewoman to draw upon, the Pine, Oak and Apple, the Feather, the Rose, Tulip and Carnation. Others were soon to be added from many different sources. Artistically speaking, this was the golden age in domestic arts and crafts. We can trace the parallel development of architecture with that of textiles and other decoration, as the fine houses were rising, and creating, as Royal Cortissoz says, "a cool, serene and handsome en-vironment" in their dignity and perfect proportions; and the life of the people gained in dignity and a sort of rich simplicity, to be worthy of the setting. Though we cannot forget the outlying settlers trembling in their beds at night listening for sounds of marauding Indians, we read of Thomas Hancock writing to London in 1738 to order some wall-paper for his house on Beacon Hill —"a shaded hanging with some Landskip at the bottom and birds flying here and there,"—a perfect description of the small hillocks of earth from which the colorful trees were to spring. He draws further upon a similar paper made for another Boston citizen, for the suggestion: "a great variety of Different sorts of Birds, Peacocks, Macoys, Squirril, Monkys, Fruit and Flowers etc." Here is the Indo-English hanging of the Jacobean Period now reduced to paper and thus spreading its influence still more widely in America.

Needleworkers could draw upon a rich variety of materials in the shops by this time, if they were within reach of the larger towns. From the files of the *Boston News-Letter* we learn that linens from Scotland, Dantzic, Russia, Polonia and Pomerania could be had, as well as "sundry sorts of silks and worsted shades, fine needles, colour'd and waxed Threads, Indigo, Scissars" and the like. We are also interested in a shop at the third door south of the Old-Brick Meeting House in Cornhill, Boston, where Dye-stuffs could be obtained: Spanish Brown, Verdegrease, Vermillion, Allum and Copperas (fixatives), Madder, Ground Red Wood and others. In spite of the political anxieties of the time, women seem to have had plenty of energy for needlework and an abiding interest in it. All this shows that we are passing from unconscious to conscious art. Primitive handwork owes much of its quality to the fact that it is made to supply some real purpose in the domestic scheme, and decorated by the same hands that prepared its materials. As soon as we begin to be able to buy designs and materials, and to copy many styles, we pass from the purposeful to the recreational, and our art becomes studied and vicarious. In the search for this purposeful simplicity and strength, we are tempted therefore to leave the more leisured ladies of the large towns sitting over their frames and carefully matching their shades, to see what was being produced in the country districts.

There were distinct differences between the American designs and the imported ones which presented "all the latest thing" in London and Paris. The chief one was, as we have said, the gain in simplicity: more space, the elimination of too profuse foliage, and simpler stitchery, so that what elaboration there was became far more telling. The American draughts-man caught something of the Chinese gift for combining masses of orna-ment with well-defined empty areas, and the clean-cut lines have a way of leading the eye along which is very agreeable. This was further ac-centuated by the peculiarly American habit of using the faithful indigo, and working the entire piece exclusively in shades of blue. After the surfeit of colors we observed in the Oriental pieces, this gives satisfying relief. There are many examples worked in a large variety of soft vege-table-dyed wools, many of which retain their brightness; but in countless cases there are three blue shades played off against each other, dark, medium and light; sometimes a fourth and fifth shade and the addition of white gives a very elaborate effect without the loss of the sharpness of outline due to the bold, clear color, and the evident certainty in the worker's mind.

All the heavy built-up stemwork of stitch upon stitch, and a mass of variegated colors and confused effects which so often characterized the English pieces was fined down to two or three rows of plain outline or chain-stitch, just heavy enough to carry the weight of the flowers. Where we have a worker with native good taste, a great number of colors and a large variety of stitches were not used on the same piece; most of the stitches were simple and effective. The wavy stem-line, or meander, which was sometimes used in England as an all-over design by running it in parallel lines like a row of growing vine stems, was mostly used in this country along borders, with a wondrous flower or leaf-spray growing in-side each curve. This wavy stem-line more or less regularly spaced off is very typical of the borders on substantial linen petticoats and on bed-valances.

The filling stitch most widely used for these flowers is that which is called in Mrs. Christie's *Samplers and Stitches* the Roumanian stitch. In this country we call it the New England stitch or Deerfield stitch, but it may equally well be called the Universal stitch, for it is found in the Scandinavian and Balkan countries, Russia and Greece and the Near East. For the purposes of this book we shall call it the Overlaid stitch as a descriptive term. The original stitch calls for a first long thread to be laid down from one outside edge of the leaf or petal to the other, and then the second process comes back across it with a sort of couching-stitch to hold it down securely. If the first stitch is extremely long, owing to the size of the area to be covered, it can be couched down with two, three or more slanting couching-stitches in its course. It allows very delicate and graceful designs to be worked, as well as bold ones, because it is so adaptable and flexible. It was often worked in rows across petals, which gave an opportunity for shading from dark to light, though not in any realistic sense. Other flower forms or parts of large flowers are filled with French knots, or separate cross-stitches used in a diaper effect, or cross-barred lines, or small seed-stitches; the outlines of the forms were chiefly in chain, outline, herring-bone and feather-stitches.

About this time, "the common ancient dress" of the men was a woollen coat, striped woollen frock (for country wear), and woollen, velvet, tow or leather breeches, with long stockings; thick cowhide shoes, and cocked hats. The more well-to-do wore wigs. The outer common dress of the women in summer was a linen gown, checked tyers or aprons; in winter, woollen gowns and aprons, thick stockings and cowhide shoes. The petti-coats and aprons were usually decorated with needlework, and there was also an essential detail on which decorative needlework could be ex-pended, in the shape of a large flat pocket worn under the skirt. This was made to tie around the waist like an apron, and was made double with a lengthwise slit which corresponded to a slit in the skirt so that the hand could reach into it easily. The tie on this bag was very often a narrow tape woven on what was called a tape-stick, usually of blue and white in a little ornamental pattern, the whole about half an inch wide but very strong. In England these were made from Queen Anne's day down to 1778, worked in several elaborate styles, even petit-point, with colored silk flowers. They were especially popular when skirts were very full and worn over a hoop. Many American pockets have survived and are worked in every degree of skill, with floral designs.

Crewel work was used to embellish bed-hangings and coverlets, chair-seats, purses and "wallets," as well as the articles previously mentioned. Another very decorative field was the needlework rug, made at great expense of time and stitchery. The design was usually floral with scrolls, and worked in bright colors. The background was then put in around it in gradually increasing supplementary lines in one color which finally met and ran together, or else a more systematic job was done and the background worked in regular rows interrupted by the design. This made a fabric not very heavy in weight for a rug, but with solid wearing qualities because of the close texture of the stitchery and the sturdy materials. The Caswell Carpet, made in Vermont in 1835 and now in the Metropolitan Museum's American Wing, is divided into small squares filled with a great variety of flower and bird motives in bright-colored wools, and is probably the finest example of a needleworked floor covering in America. We find many small domestic articles which show signs of having been part of such a rug; probably the unworn parts were cut out and made into wallets, small bags and mats.

Another American development was a triple form, met with over and over again, where three flowers or foliate forms of equal size whose stems unite into one, spring from a scroll or a shell-shape. As the main emphasis in this motive comes at the stem-ends, it forms itself naturally within the unseen lines of a square or diamond. Small triple sprays of this kind were often used as a scatter design between larger sprays, but the form remains typical.

The shell was appearing in wood carving, at the tops of highboys and the curved tops of corner cupboards, and there are shell shapes for some reason on early tombstones. Perhaps the introduction of this design came in with the marine curios brought home in merchant ships. It found its way into the quaint pages of little books of cross-stitch patterns, and thence to footstool tops worked on canvas; and later Martha Washington used it in embroidering her famous chair-seats.

A particularly graceful and interesting piece bearing the name of Miriam Webb is dated 1756. It is part of a set of bed-hangings, worked on white linen in colored crewels, and the valance has a wavy stem-line from which grow the carnation, scalloped ferny leaves, fanciful flora and berries. Miss Marian Hague in commenting on these pieces in the Bulletin of the Needle and Bobbin Club says:

They make us wonder how these colonial embroiderers in isolated settlements, as well as in the larger sea coast towns, developed such a distinct style. Of course they had brought some patterns and traditions with them from the Old Country and they certainly used the printed India cottons as inspirations for details, but even so it is interesting to see what a sisterhood of workers there must have been. . . . Miriam Webb used a lovely crimson dye (madder?) with lighter tones of pink, a clear yellow, and two greens which seem to have lasted very well, besides many shades of blue, a tan, grays and a gold color.

A pleasant habit persists in the country of women bringing their sewing for an afternoon together, comparing designs and new styles of work; and it is probable that in 1750 they did the same, perhaps gathering around one leading figure who was more skilled or more inventive than the rest. Such interesting pieces have been found in Keene, New Hampshire, for instance, made by several different hands, that a little needlework center must have existed there, and the same is probably true in many districts in other states. This neighborly rivalry could well be called a "sisterhood of workers," with community of ideas.

Another very fine dated piece is that worked by Mary Bulman in 1745, now in York, Maine. The central area of the bed-cover is filled by eight large motives, the corner ones being trees with fruit, and the others large flowering plants of equal size; a little running vine crosses between them. The unique thing about this set of bed-furnishings is that the maker combined two thoughts in introducing into her crewel work some pious verses resembling those much in vogue on cross-stitch samplers.

This gives us an opening to consider the religious influence in general. It was the sampler more than the crewel pieces which became the vehicle for religious expression, in verses of hymns and moral advice to the young; and later the names of patchwork bedquilt-patterns reflected the same influences. The piety of our ancestors which was one of the motives of their migration ran very strongly along Puritan and Protestant lines. They fed upon Fox's *Book of Martyrs*, John Bunyan's *Pilgrim's Progress*, they studied the Old Testament, particularly its more cheerless aspects, and they sang peculiarly blood-curdling hymns about death, dissolution and the judgment of a lost and dying race. The sense of original sin weighed them down—"Nor running brook, nor flood, nor sea can wash the dismal stain away." Indigo blue seemed to be their spiritual color as well as the one most frequent in their surroundings. During the fanatical witchcraft incidents in Salem in 1690 and after, we find that crosses were introduced into door-panellings as a protective measure, or at least so runs the legend; but not many other crosses were to be found in New England, as they savored of Popery. Hearts and stars and crowns may have had religious significance, coming vaguely down from the centuries of European Catholic symbolism, as well as the Tree of Life and the stag. The grapevine which is constantly used almost certainly had a religious meaning, for no such earnest students of the scriptures as our ancestors were likely to miss the verse, "I am the Vine, ye are the branches," and the very many other references to it. The popular design of a bird, often identifiable as the mourning dove or turtle dove which was common to all the New England states, bearing a small spray of leaves or berries in its beak, has been considered by some thinkers to be the dove who flew back to the Ark bearing the olive twig; and inasmuch as this carries a promise, as a rainbow lightens a stormy sky, we welcome it as a hopeful sign. It was the fashion then to be melancholy; but we like to think that in the crewel work, with its bright colors and designs taken more and more from nature, we have a true reflection of the maker's normal, healthy point of view, her blossoming garden and the birds and animals which inhabited it, and the homely cheer of her hospitable house.

A thoroughly cheerful example is the bed-cover illustrated, with "divers sorts" of trees, some of which look like pattern-book designs, and others almost certainly being original. Its history is not known, as it was bought at an auction from a New England dealer's collection. The blossoming thistle, lifelike sprays of barberries and currants and the butterflies and other details are very well drawn, interspersed with less shapely forms; the apple tree in the lower right-hand corner has been slightly crowded by a grapevine which winds awkwardly upward. The most interesting detail of this piece is the brook, worked in overlapping waves in two shades of blue in a very original manner, which has unmistakable brook trout swimming upon its surface, their gray sides mottled with red and gold spots. This seems to suggest a picture based on a real place or event rather than on a pattern book.

Another good example is the valance with deer and fish, and sundry leaves and flowers along a wavy stem-line. This piece has two original bits of detail that suggest some taste for nature study; one is the red-winged blackbird in flight, New England's authentic harbinger of spring, and the other some creditable raspberries worked in deep rose thread in bullion stitch as a variant from the nondescript fruits which are variously called currants, mountain ash, grapes, and bittersweet in the old china patterns.

But for the alertness of a friend, the tablecloth in Fig. 13 might never have reached the public view. As we study the simple design outlined in stone-colored thread, we are minded to quote the poem, "This is good New England rock, rooted in earth from which it grew," for this piece is as primitive, austere and beautifully clean as the little rock-ribbed hill farm from which it came. Woven in two breadths and seamed down the middle, it is worked in unbleached gray linen thread which was raised from flax, spun and wrought into stitches by the same hands. This is an individual piece, with a carefully worked edge of loops of the same gray thread. The present owner is nearly a hundred years old, and I am grateful to her for allowing this ancestral piece to be photographed.

If one lived in the vicinity of good shops, it was possible to buy "Sattin or Canvis" prepared for embroidering, with ready-made patterns in any desired subject. But the sisterhood in the country evidently did their own pattern transferring. An examination of many old pieces shows the design drawn on with a faded brownish ink which looks like berry juice or an infusion of bark, as washing has spread the stain. For the large pieces like needle-worked rugs, the method used later in the hooked rugs of cutting out scrolls and flowers and other large forms from stiff paper and drawing around them with pointed charcoal was probably employed. This has the merit of allowing the designer to plan out the area by actually laying the shapes upon it and moving them about until the effect is wholly satisfactory. A large kit of such cut-out motives has recently come to light in an attic which must have been hoarded by several generations, and has, besides the separate forms, long sections of border-lines, cut out or traced, such as the cable, which can be laid down and outlined on the fabric.

The flowers themselves were the beloved carnation, the tulip, rose, campanula or bell-flower, a composite five-petalled blossom probably descended from the potato blossom with its pointed petals and elongated pistil; and incidental to them all, the Oriental palm leaf or "Persian pine." Designers were growing more garden-minded as time went on. Styles which once gained a hold, however, changed slowly, and many Oriental details still survive, as a study of the illustrations plainly shows. These people who were ushering their family's future homesteads into the world largely by hand let their fancy play. They took names directly from nature for their patterns and designs: the gooseneck andirons, the duck-foot tables, the honeycomb moulding, the scattered leaf pattern on the rug. There was also the pomegranate bursting with seeds, which was naturally the symbol of plenty and richness, and the pineapple with its prickly leaves opening wide to disclose the heart within was the symbol of hospitality to be carved on gateposts and over many a doorway.

The finest draughtsmanship which I know of, for natural ease, grace and accuracy, occurs in the designs for some curtains embroidered in 1786 by Elizabeth Hartwell of Edgartown, Mass., and presumably drawn by her. In the copies of these eight or ten floral designs which the present owner in Keene, N. H., allowed me to make, it is shown how very clearly the stitches are indicated and the use of the three shades of blue in which the entire set was to be worked. It was difficult to choose two out of the group, for illustrating here.

Another very fine set of bed-furniture now owned in North Easton, Mass., is also in blue and white, but is given a wonderful feeling of delicacy by using a minimum of solidly filled forms, and by working an outward-turning buttonhole-stitch in white around every motive. This set employs the triple spray in several sizes (see Fig. 9) and has some very Chinese birds on the bed-curtains. There is great variety here, as if the worker took pleasure in inventing small differences.

Two workers in Hatfield, Mass., Rebecca Dickinson and Polly Wright, wrought a bed-cover in 1763 and departed entirely from the prevalent tree form, building a large central figure around crossed sections of wavy stem. There are many more beautiful examples, some crude, some beautifully done, and all different even though the component motives may be very similar.

The final struggle between France and England, into which the colonies had been drawn, was decided in 1759, and England's attempts to recoup herself by squeezing the colonies began in earnest. With the growing feeling against the mother country which culminated with the Stamp Act, a new and independent stand was to be taken which would throw the colonists back upon their own resources again for a time. Congress met in October, 1765, and drew up a Declaration of Rights, which amounted to a boycott. Merchants agreed not to buy British goods, and citizens pledged themselves to wear homespun clothes and to do without imported luxuries. Once more looms began to thump and spinning wheels to hum, and New Englanders went back into homespun with righteous ardor. The embroidery craze probably had to wait a little on necessity, for the clothing problem was again paramount.

In 1750, as trade was beginning to fall off, several spinning schools had been opened in Boston to encourage the manufacture of native linen cloth even in the large towns where this craft had ceased to be practised during the prosperous years. People were urged in the newspapers to send their children to learn this useful art. In 1753 the Massachusetts Court made an appropriation to encourage the work further, because "by the great decay of Trade and Business the number of Poor is greatly increased and the burden of supporting them lies heavy on many of the towns within this Province." The fear of Indian raids over a long period had something to do with this overcrowding of the towns; some of the weaker brethren had lost their taste for pioneering in the wilds and had given up the struggle, and there were surviving relatives of the slain who, having lost all they owned, were now dependent. In the old histories of the small New England towns, many of which were hidden among the hills and out of touch

[44]

for long periods, there were evidences of the slowly rising indignation of the country people. One little village in New Hampshire sends forty bushels of rye "to the Poor of ye Town of Boston," out of its own none too plentiful store. The old village chronicles are homespun histories indeed.

We who remember the World War know what patriotic fervor can be kindled by martial events, and troubles leading up to the outbreak of the Revolution were growing very disquieting. In 1766 the "Daughters of Liberty" in Providence had all-day spinning meetings to provide the president and graduating class at Rhode Island College with homespun suits for Commencement, and Harvard's supporters did the same. Women gave up their interest in the European fashions and led in the determination to be self-supporting. The beautiful bed-cover worked by Mary Breed, which is now in the Metropolitan Museum's American wing, is dated 1770, and is rich in well drawn designs, many of which are quite individual, such as the strange fanlike formation which terminates the trunk of the central tree in whose branches roost, not one, but a whole flock of pigeons. As it was customary to mark the date when a piece was finished, we cannot guess how long Mary Breed, "aged nineteen," had been at work on her masterpiece. The embroidered pieces of this time are getting well away from the Jacobean type which does not reappear, the only thing they have in common being the general subject of growing things and birds and an occasional deer.

Perhaps New England "went in all over" with its customary spirit, for in 1774, John Adams writes in his carefully kept diary, "Took our departure in a very great rain from the happy, the peaceful, the elegant, the hospitable and polite city of Philadelphia." The return to New England seems to have been made with a wistful look behind him, for Boston at this time was beginning to seethe and could not be called happy or peaceful. The Boston Tea Party had occurred in 1773, drawing forth the following bit of fancy from Mercy Warren, one of Mrs. Adams's correspondents:

> Now all the watery dames [water nymphs?]
> May snuff souchong, and sip, in flowing bowls,
> The higher flavored choice Hysonian stream,
> And leave their nectar to old Homer's gods.

We quote this, not only to show that even now some could take a lighter view of this serious time, but as an indicative forerunner of the classical turn which New England was soon to take. Excavations at Pompeii and Herculaneum had been going on, and Robert Adam, a Scottish architect, was just now the King's architect on the Board of Works and popularizing his classical studies in London. Boston, as the Athens of America, would be one of the first places for these seeds to take root as soon as she had time, and was adept at intellectual play. But that was not yet, for we are in the midst of Revolutionary manifestations of a serious character. The war had really begun, and Mr. Adams writes anxiously to his wife, "In case of real danger, fly to the woods with our children."

Every schoolchild who has studied his country's history is familiar with the sequence of events, from the ride of Paul Revere to the surrender of Cornwallis in 1781. Some say that the stars and stripes of our flag were first suggested by the Washington family's coat of arms, the bars and the three stars across the shield which is carved in stone at Sulgrave Manor. Others deny this. Without mixing in the quarrel, we will simply mention the fact that the flag first hoisted over St. Leger's camp in the primeval forest of Oneida County was made of scraps of a blue jacket, a white shirt, and red flannel (source uncertain), and its design was adopted by Congress in 1777. Stars and eagles became very numerous in every form from that time on, from ship's figure-heads to bedquilts. The eagle is a bird of proud and fiery temper and has been the emblem of many conquerors; and though a royal bird, is now the symbol of American democracy. The flag which was carried up Bunker Hill bore the pine tree as its device.

A sampler of this time, now owned in Charlestown, Mass., shows the British red-coats ascending the steeps of Bunker Hill, an abruptly rising mound, and coming down crushed and broken on the other side. This same subject is treated vigorously on some bed-curtains worked in crewels, now exhibited in the Brooklyn Museum (see Fig. 1); the sequence of events seems to run from the bottom, where the British ranks are led by mounted officers, up a sharp incline with guns on shoulders, in the middle section, and falling back in complete disarray in the top corner.

It is difficult to hold strictly to the subject of crewel work when so many allied branches of textile decoration illustrate so clearly the public mind. The names of bedquilt patterns are some of the straws which showed how the wind was blowing. There was Burgoyne Surrounded, a quilt worked out in dark blue rectangles said to be taken from an actual plan of the battle, regiments being represented on military plans as small black blocks. There was the Tea Leaf, and many forms of the Star, and it was a significant change when the pattern known as Queen Charlotte's Crown was renamed the Indian Spring.

America went through troublous times and severe privations before her independence was won, and the needles of the women recorded them on sampler and quilt and bed-cover. Washington's "homespun army" wore homemade uniforms which in some cases were reduced from the raw material to the garment in record time. The colors were sometimes butternut brown, but the popular designation was "blue and buff." The blue was home-dyed indigo in a great many cases. Buff is defined by the dictionary as a "dull deep yellow," and the combination is the same one which speaks to us from the crewel embroideries, for from this time saffron yellow and fustic yellow are introduced among the blue and white. We have it again in the bedquilts, deep blue on one side and saffron yellow on the other, quilted with the tulip and the feather, which seem to be a peculiarly New Hampshire product. Of the dozen or so which I have run across, every one traces back to New Hampshire; and this patriotic combination seems to have originated in the Richardson family in Protectworth, later called Springfield, N. H. These deep, honest colors of the hold-fast type suggest to this day that shabby army with broken shoes; and the unique garment discovered very recently in a country attic bears out this impression. It is a blue homespun wool coat upon whose breast is stitched the Purple Heart bestowed by Washington himself for valor, and it might have been cut off the same piece as Moses Richardson's quilts, so similar is it in texture.

Country craftsmen in every line picked up their designs wherever they found them, even as you and I. They had the advantage of us in being able to see possibilities in simpler, more natural things, being undistracted by the medley of outside sources and by the smattering of many periods which are brought to us in so many ways. All their handicrafts, therefore, are closely related. The same designs, or at least the same motives, reappear on carved furniture, engraved teaspoons, wall-papers, rugs and chintzes. Gravestones in peaceful old country cemeteries often prove a rich field for the student, once we have got past the skull and crossbones era. This is particularly true of the Revolutionary cemetery at Old Bennington, Vermont, which has some really lovely floral designs on its stones. The Fassett stone, dated 1782, and the Dewey stone, 1790, make us wonder whether the engraver had a notable needlewoman among his female relations, thus being familiar with Trees of Life, floral wavy stems and baskets of fruit with graceful foliated tendrils, or whether—as seems more unlikely—needlewomen from far and near drew on his achievements with the chisel for their designs!

There is one more important contribution to needlework of just this time, which although not strictly crewel work is hard to classify in any other way. This is a type of bed-cover worked on a woollen fabric in heavy wool threads, in huge floral designs. It is almost always in buff and blue, running off into tan and greenish variations characteristic of vegetable colorings. All of these bed-covers whose history is known can be definitely placed as from the Connecticut valley. At first sight the work looks like hooking, but in the specimen now in the Currier Gallery of Art in Manchester, N. H., it is quite plainly done with a needle in darning or running stitch in several strands of thread, the stitches running round and round in rows which fill up the entire form. The one illustrated here is dated 1771, and others which were pictured in the *Antiques Magazine* for November, 1934, all date between 1790 and 1798. The colors and the general design are allied to the crewel pieces, but the coarse, heavy stitchery suggests a rug. Perhaps this was a local type developed by a "sisterhood" of needlewomen in the valley, which never attained renown elsewhere.

The end of the Revolutionary time came at last, and saw the end of America's parochial period, for when the country recovered and began to take a place among the world's independent nations, things were never the same. Another fifty years of interesting needlework from our point of view were ahead, but the workers began before long to lose confidence in their own ideas, and strength gradually declined into mere gentility. What is worse, the American failing of being in a hurry began to be reflected in the work. The patient use of leisure time by which the tapestry pieces and large, important furnishings had been covered, stitch by stitch, gives way more and more to broader effects, with an effort to cover the ground by quicker means, and this was to bring in a different feeling and a new technique. The Golden Age of our native needlework was over.

THE RISING SUN

✦✦

NEW ENGLAND, from its tree-clad northern slopes to its front on the Atlantic Ocean, is like a tiny model on which the rest of America is formed, an inch to a mile. Here are the mountains, black forests and deep ravines, the rivers, broad fields and stony hillsides, the sand dunes and salt marshes, which, hugely magnified, make up the vast areas of this country. And as it is concentrated in size, so it is in history, tradition, character. Its flavor is like one of its own apples: not so large as others, perhaps, but with a redder cheek, a more spicy edge. Men who live close to nature, dependent on her slow changes, are also slow to change. They have something of the gradual growth and unfolding of a tree, and the grain at heart is in a secret pattern; they strike deep roots. Cut away the little surface roots and runners, and they can still draw life from something farther down.

If we travel up across the New England states today, there are many districts in which, by eliminating in fancy a few details such as cement roads and telegraph poles, we can still see the homes of the people as they were at the end of the Revolution. Over the slope of a hill the broad, comfortable gable comes into view; the huge central chimney with a feather of smoke; the gray barns and fences, the ageless lilacs and apple trees, the roadside clumps of orange lilies and the Queen Anne's lace. We can picture the women who lived there when the house was new, sitting in the window with needle in hand, letting their fancy dictate small details to set into the design for their own amusement and pleasure—a bird flying by, a flower growing under the window. This is what has given their work its individuality, as it incorporated the Eastern strain of the period into its own local usage. It is no more surprising to find a pomegranate or a palmette in their needleworked pieces than to picture them drinking tea out of blue cups from China, or wearing an India shawl to meeting.

Mary Ellen Chase has drawn a vivid picture of the old deep-sea families along the coast in her stories of American captains and their wives who accompanied them sometimes on the long voyages. Many an old house in the seaboard towns has a sea-going flavor to this day: a portrait of a man in brass buttons, with massive front, a curled forelock, one stern eye and one twinkling one—perhaps the picture was painted in Bremen or Cadiz. There is a little ship in a bottle, too, an intricate piece of carving betokening the long days at sea; an ostrich egg decorated with crossed cannon, an eagle, and the motto "Let Liberty Reign!" beneath the Stars and Stripes. These country homes with their habit of hoarding things have been chiefly instrumental in saving the treasures of the past for us. Alas, primitive attics grow more hard to find with every passing year, and the spring cleaning done by "pizen-neat" housekeepers has very much to answer for in the destruction or dispersing of priceless relics. In the cities, changes in the mode of life and the itch to follow the latest fashion have done their part as well; many fine houses and public buildings were pulled down as business encroached or withdrew. It is in the old country homes that we stand the best chance of finding what remains intact; many of them still stand firm. They were built for the future.

They seldom had a professional architect, for the custom was to call upon the local builder who used a reference book, or his own collection of measured drawings made from what he had seen or worked out himself. He usually had at his command the *Builder's Bench-Mate*, or some similar handbook: Inigo Jones on the works of the Italian Andrea Palladio, accounted the greatest architect of the late Renaissance in the land of his birth, or Asher Benjamin, who wrote the first American original work, *The Country Builder's Assistant*, in 1797. We must also mention again a name which had a very strong influence on American homes: that of Robert Adam. He is important to us because he not only built houses, but evolved a whole school of decoration and furniture to go inside them, making the whole an artistic unit—the forerunner of the modern interior decorator whose periods must be historically accurate and complete. Robert was the creative mind, evidently, of the four Adam brothers. Extensive travels in Europe had opened for him the classical Orders which he studied minutely. From his careful measurements and sketches of Greek and Roman buildings, the brothers published a book of plates, not only of large conceptions but of the minutest details of what they considered to be necessary parts of a harmonious whole, ideally complete, even into the realm of garden ornaments. The last remaining remnant of the heavy Tudor usage in England gave way to these charming and graceful new creations, and with his structural lines he brought in the Italian decorative subjects of wreaths and garlands, urns, arrows, and mythical animals which we associate with his name. The columbine, a favorite motive of his, began to bloom in English embroideries, though its long spurs presented difficulties for amateur draughtsmen. In time this vogue came to America, and there is hardly a fine house of the end of the eighteenth century which has not a trace of him in spacious proportions, mantelpiece, mirror or moulding. Here was a definite instance of America tapping the "Time-stream" from the East.

So far we have had largely in mind the houses of the well-to-do residents in the larger towns and along the seacoast, who were participants

ILLUSTRATIONS

FIGURE 1. The Battle of Bunker Hill on a bed-curtain.
British Soldiers in crewel wools, c. 1776

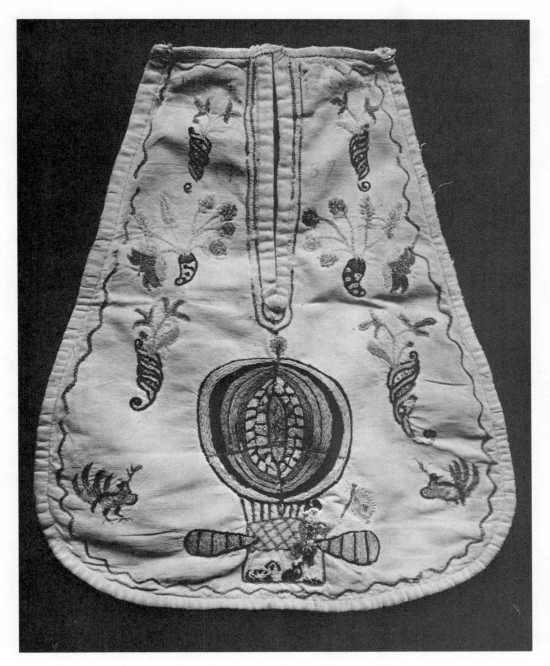

FIGURE 2. A balloon ascension, 1784, embroidered on a linen pocket

FIGURE 3. A version of the Italian artichoke from Acworth, N. H.

FIGURE 4. The Rose worked by Mary Breed, 1770

FIGURE 5. A running stag and an oak-tree, and a pine

FIGURE 6. A pocket worked with tulip, clover and carnation

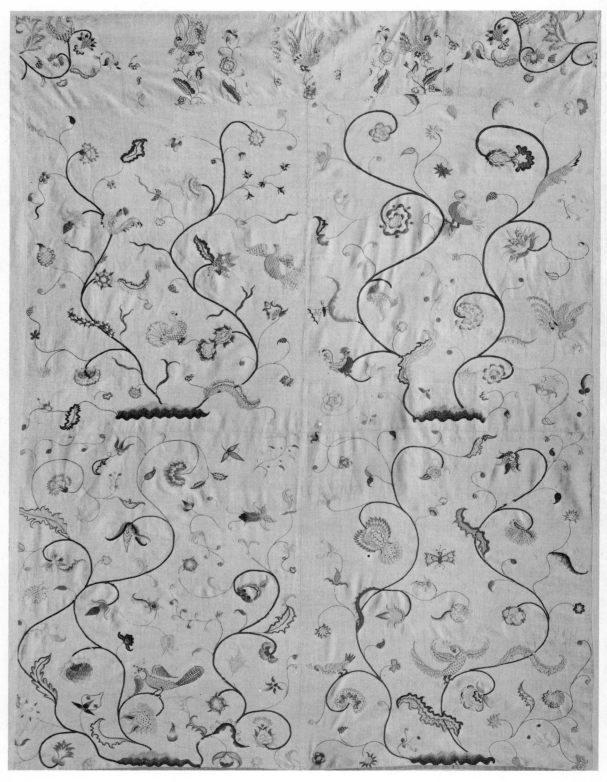

FIGURE 7. Oriental birds, and roses, thistles, etc., growing from a Chinese wave, a medley of influences

FIGURE 8. Corner of a rug worked entirely in overlaid stitches in many colors

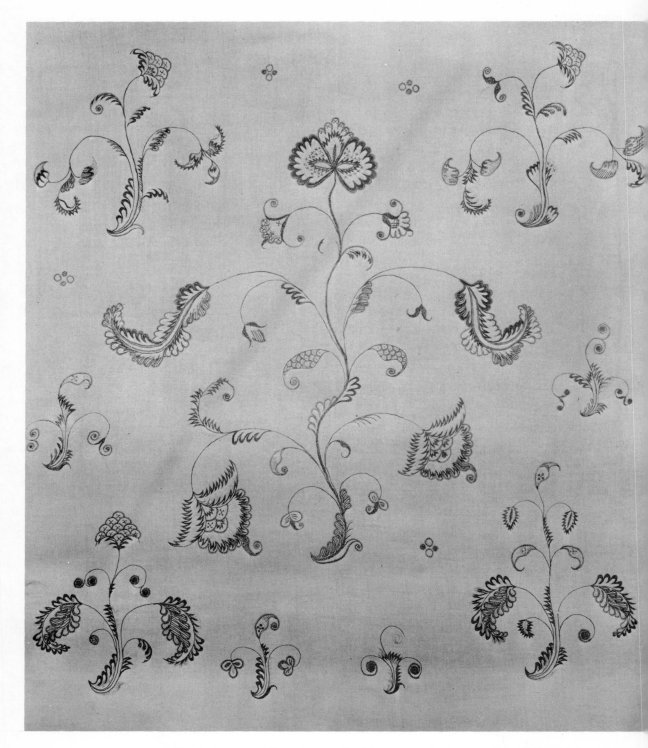

FIGURE 9. Triple sprays delicately worked in three shades of blue and white

FIGURE 10. Various fruit trees, berries and flowers which suggest a pattern book, with original additions

FIGURE 11. Detail of border, FIGURE 10. A trout-brook with waves in two shades of blue

FIGURE 12. A wavy stem-line on a valance, with stag, red-winged blackbird, and raspberries

FIGURE 13. A table-cover worked by Lois Chandler, born in 1794, with a well-balanced design, and the Rising Sun in corners

FIGURE 14. Drawings from blue and white curtains made by Elizabeth Hartwell

FIGURE 15. Wool-on-wool bed-cover in darning stitch from the Connecticut Valley

FIGURE 16. The Sewall blanket, a compendium of American design, dating about the end of the Revolution

FIGURE 17. The American Scene: a needle-worked picture

FIGURE 18. Indian-printed cotton palampore, familiar in American homes, with Persian Pine, and wavy-stem borders

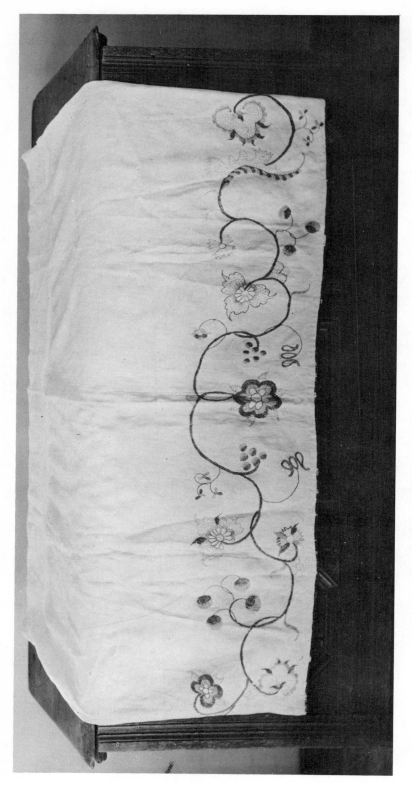

FIGURE 19. Linen petticoat with blue-and-white border. Below the central rose are two columbine flowers

FIGURE 20. A reconstruction by the author of a table-cover in three blues, Prince's Feather, Rose of Sharon, carnation, bunches of currants and grapes

FIGURE 21. Design by Elizabeth Hartwell of Edgartown, Massachusetts, 1786, in three shades of blue

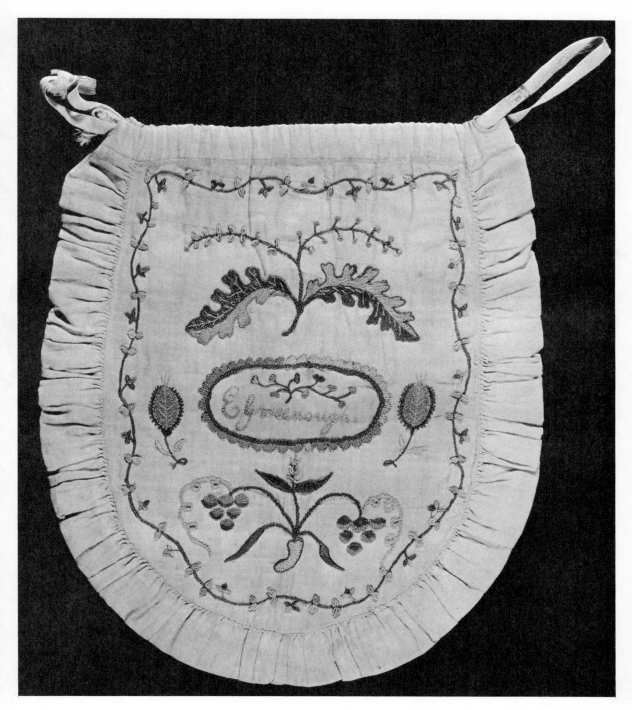

FIGURE 22. Small linen bag worked in silks by Eliza Greenough

FIGURE 23. A linen holder with a delicate bit of draftsmanship

FIGURE 24. A group of Deerfield pieces with characteristic flowers, and the bee and thistle

FIGURE 25. A well-designed modern piece of fine workmanship

FIGURE 26. A motif from Mary's Breed's coverlet (1770). A good piece of planning, strong stem lines, use of stitches

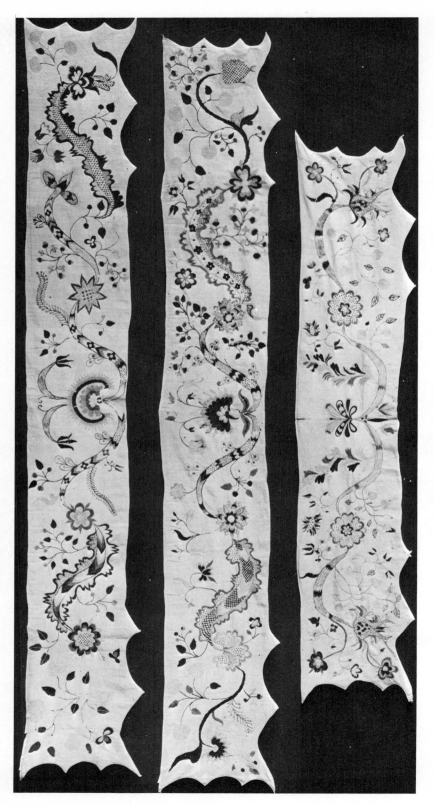

FIGURE 27. A set of bed valances. An example of old-time stitchery, in shades of blue

FIGURE 28. Four adaptations of designs from old china, a jug
and other New England sources

FIGURE 29. Triple sprays from a Topsfield, Mass. coverlet
adapted on a modern piece in blue and gold

FIGURE 30. Detail of coverlet, wool on linen. The large flower is a typical example of the overlaid stitch

FIGURE 31. Bed hangings in the Garrison house, Exeter, N. H.
The top valance was reconstructed from a fragment of the original

in national and world affairs during the years of our growing commerce and increasing wealth. But comfortable living was by no means confined to these families. The dwellers in the interior affirmed then, as now, their equal right to possess and enjoy all needful things and follow the popular fashions. Men lived on their own acres with their sons and daughters around them to assist in building the family fortunes, and their riches were real and tangible: big barns and herds and rich crops from fertile fields. Perhaps in the realm of needlework the country people had the advantage, for they lived nearer to nature which was still the chief source of materials. We are tempted to say that crewel embroidery reached its best flowering in the hands of the country workers, because of their independence of spirit. Certainly they have left us some extremely interesting pieces. They were not so prone to copy, nor so easily influenced by every change of fashion, and their work gained by it in strength and simplicity.

An English writer of today says:

Democracy as we know it in this country (England) is a country product.... It flourished again, as perhaps never before or since, in the early pioneer days of Anglo-Saxon North America ... a conception of democracy which grew up in our English fields, and was transplanted across the Atlantic. The man who lives with the freedom of his own plot of mother earth about him is born lord to a certain independence ... the proudest creature living, and I think the happiest.*

Wall-papers came to America first about 1735, and were naturally all the fashion among those who could afford them. One of the oldest designs in Chinese hand-painted papers was a series of little scenes showing the tea-growing industry. Perhaps it was from this idea of scenic repeats that the French and English makers were soon picturing all sorts of incidents, historic or playful, from the first balloon ascension to the shepherdesses of the Petit Trianon, from Washington in triumph (to

*Arthur Bryant, in the *Illustrated London News*, 1938.

[53]

tempt American pocket-books) to the game of hide and seek. For the simpler homes where the cost of these lovely papers was prohibitive, there was some one to copy them in spirit by actual paintings on the plaster, and we have many quaint and amusing murals which show the Yankee inventiveness for meeting a demand. The needleworkers were making pictures too; but the petit-point of the former type was slow, and larger stitches were used, sometimes helped out with paints.

Another expensive fashion at this time was the Kashmir shawl. During the reign of Napoleon as Emperor of the French, genuine Kashmir shawls from Srinagar became the vogue in Paris. They were made in Kashmir, a native state of India lying at the northern end of the Himalaya Mountains, and were made of countless tiny bits of colored wool fabric welded together by stitches of fairylike fineness into one large piece of material. They took years to make, and cost from one to five hundred dollars, so that only the wealthy could afford them. To meet this situation, the weavers in Paisley, Scotland, a famous textile town, were soon making a woven imitation, quite different in texture as they came from the loom all in one piece, but of similar design and soft, pleasant colorings. These succeeded very well in effect, at a much more reasonable figure, and were widely popular in America. There is hardly an attic which has not either a real India shawl—thanks to some sea-going ancestor—or a Paisley shawl laid away; and as the Paisleys have long since ceased to be woven, they too will become with the passage of time as important an heirloom as their richer prototypes. Both had their influence in familiarizing New Englanders with the Eastern designs and colorings; the palmette or "Persian pine" was constantly seen.

Another source of interest which took its place in many homes was the Oriental rug. Its importation must have brought with it useful hints to designers and especially to colorists, as we see in the early printed cotton dress-materials. In the Near East, yarns for rugs are produced from sheep's wool today by the same process as for our own primitive textiles, and dyed with natural dyes. I have often seen in Turkey those soft pools of color spread out on the grass to dry after a thorough washing in pure water. There was a special place outside the walls of Constantinople where a grassy slope in the full glare of the sun was always spread with rugs drying under the care of a man who turned them from time to time. This was the trial by fire, so to speak, which proved a genuine antique rug; for the old ones did not fade, but only grew more soft and beautiful in the cleansing, while the modern, chemically dyed copies would run together and fade in blotches. A customer had a right to demand that a rug be washed, and an upright merchant would not fear to take the challenge. The wearing qualities were almost endless, for the Eastern makers used sound materials and knew every secret of their art. When the American trading ships returning from the Levant brought them in, new artistic influences came with them.

These "tall ships" which shuttled back and forth across the world wove many strands into the fabric of New England life. In many of the coast towns, especially during the great activity in the shipyards which were turning out all types of vessels for the growing foreign trade, there were remarkable ship-carvers and wood-workers, who could carve a panel or ornamental door-frame as well as a ship's figurehead. To their skilled hands we owe many an eagle and shell and dolphin. Over Portsmouth doors and mantels there are dolphins, and in them we have a fusing of elements. The dolphin was one of the mythical sea-beasts, with a great affection for mariners; Pliny wrote centuries ago that "of himselfe he meeteth their ships, playeth and disporteth himselfe, and fetcheth a thousand friskes and gambols before them." During the Stuart intrigues it was used as the symbol of the Dauphin, a rather obvious one, it would seem—who took his title from the French province of Dauphiné. We prefer to think that the sailor who carved the Portsmouth ones was thinking of the porpoises, beloved of seamen, which came wheeling out to escort his ship past Gibraltar into the Mediterranean, or of the heavy brass and silver door-knockers which decorate every door in Lisbon and Malta.

The symbol which came closest to expressing the high hopes of America at this time received its commission from Benjamin Franklin. In John Fiske's account of the Federal Convention the incident is thus described:

On the back of the president's quaint black armchair there was emblazoned a half-sun, brilliant with its gilded rays. As the meeting was breaking up and Washington arose, Franklin pointed to the chair, and made it the text for prophecy. "As I have been sitting here all these weeks," he said, "I have often wondered whether yonder sun is setting or rising. But now I know that it is a rising sun."

From that moment, the Rising Sun meant the young Republic, whose strength and energy were just beginning to ascend. On the little Sewall blanket we have it, worked in saffron and indigo, with the bright half uppermost, and rays surrounding it. This piece of much mended woollen homespun is a compendium of American design in itself. Probably done about the end of the Revolution, it carries motives that represent the whole period of America's entity. Here are the Tudor rose, the oak leaf and grapes from England; the carnation and the pomegranate, and the suggestion of the plant springing from the earth's orb, of India; the Chinese wave-form; the dove with a sprig in its beak, and the bleeding-heart, bunch of currants, daisy and clover from the American out-of-doors, and the significant little rising sun worked between the scalloped divisions of the whole border. The family initial, a winged S, completes one corner.

A beautifully worked linen tablecover in three shades of blue also dates to about this time; but it is in such ruins from long wear and abuse

The Rising Sun, from a partially-worked needlework picture

that the design is almost lost, and it was only reproduced after minute study of half-obliterated lines and ragged stitches. Its design consists of two motives, a corner and a side figure, which taken together build up a rather noble design of grapes, currants, carnations and roses. In this piece, there are rayed circles on stems, and as the years go on there still survived the rayed disk, although it became confused with the berries and other garden forms until its makers probably lost sight of its origin. The circle surrounded by little points was another way of working the rayed sun, and this occurs in several of the illustrations, for example in the tablecover worked in unbleached linen thread. (Fig. 13.)

A curious piece which was lent me in Exeter for examination tells such a story of a sequence of events that it is worth describing in detail. On one side of a 22-inch square of stout brown homespun there is a carefully drawn design, evidently prepared by a professional, only a small part of which has been worked. Three trees take up the upper half, an oak, apple and poplar (?). Under the oak, in whose branches sits a giant squirrel, a lady is pensively listening to a man playing on a shepherd's pipe. Among the little hillocks at her feet are large roses and buds, strawberries, a thistle, clover and star-shaped flowers and berry sprays, a huge lily and pomegranate, and there is a small pond with two swans upon very wriggly little waves, and birds and butterflies. The costumes and attitudes suggest that it was based on the scenes found in French wall-papers, and there is nothing very noteworthy about it. The apple tree has been almost completed in bright colors in petit-point, the texture of the background being so fine that the stitches are minute.

But on the reverse side is a more interesting design, drawn crudely in brown ink which has run and blotted in places. A large branching tree is the central figure, with Chinese flowers copied with exactness from the familiar designs on china. Beneath it stand a large lady and gentleman in costumes of about 1775, such as we see in Copley's portraits: she in a stiffly boned bodice and full skirt, wearing a cap and carrying a fan, and he in knee breeches and buckled shoes, and a wig. In the upper left corner a rayed sun is shining down on two other ladies who are balanced precariously on their heels, and beneath them is a two-storied house with smoke pouring out of its chimney. The rest of the space is filled in by a deer, dogs, birds and strawberry plants. The four human figures suggest by their awkwardness that the artist was unpractised, but they have a curious air of directness and reality. Each side of this piece has been partly worked, with such confused results that it could not be photographed, and the design could only be taken off by pricking; but from this welter of ink and stitches, we can guess at the intending worker's line of thought. The first design, possibly an imported one, looked very large indeed to be filled in with petit-point, and the needlewoman grew disheartened and put it away. At a later date the linen was brought out again and a larger, more spontaneous conception was drawn on and begun in overlaid stitch, which is a good space-filler and gets over the ground with more speed. But we shall never know whether the sun was drawn as a patriotic manifestation of the loyal American spirit, or in reminiscence of a certain sunny morning in an Exeter garden. It gives us to see, however, a piece of work just as its owner dropped it unfinished, a hundred and fifty years ago.

Pieces of crewel embroidery of this time show a complete range of colors, even to the violet and mulberry shades which had been so fugitive. A delicate violet could be had from the iris, as well as various blends, and these have come down relatively unfaded in several of the pieces illustrated.

Silks were being used now, on bags and samplers, and some of these silk threads show signs of having been ravelled from textiles. This thrifty habit was used by Martha Washington herself, as it is told that she saved her worn silk dresses, ravelled and redyed the silk and wound it on bobbins for various uses.

At the turn of the century, there were samplers with the alphabets worked in the orthodox cross-stitch, but with a panel of crewel-worked flowers introduced across the bottom, as if the makers were becoming impatient with the more tedious method of counting threads. Young ladies attended female academies, and were set to painting flowers, to darning on lace net, as at the very famous Female Academy of Miss Pierce in Litchfield, Connecticut, and to stencilling on velvet, as well as making samplers. With all these accomplishments, they were ceasing to be original, for there were rigid conventions. The task was set by a teacher, who usually started the work. In the case of pictures with figures, which were now becoming the mode—Columbia with a horn of plenty, and the like—the faces and flesh tints were painted in, and the needleworked portions reduced to a border or to the plainer parts and outlines. Thus we have the needle picture of former times, when it resembled a tapestry with the entire area covered with stitches, descending to the level of a water-color sketch with embroidered accessories. An old *Manual of Needle-work* condemns the practice in the following righteous words:

In working a landscape, some recommend the placing behind the canvas a painted sky, to avoid the trouble of working one. As a compliance with such advice would tend to foster habits of idleness and deception, and thus weaken that sense of moral propriety which should, in all we do, be ever present with us, as well as destroy that nice sense of honor and sincerity which flies from every species of deceit, we hope the votaries of this delightful art will reject the suggestion with the contempt it deserves.

This is getting far away from the crewel work which is the original theme of our study, and it will be seen that the decline had set in. Times were changing, and other interests multiplying, and many new varieties of handwork were engaging the feminine attention. Patchwork bed-quilts were growing increasingly popular, and rugs of wool or rag strips hooked into heavy linen crash. These were both forms of decoration by which a pattern could be built up with more speed and less detail, much to the disadvantage of the older type, which called for the laborious placing of careful stitches.

Washington, who had been the unanimous choice of the nation for President, died in 1799, leaving an orphan country behind him. Mourning was expressed not only in lengthy sermons and odes, but by artists in every medium, who depicted it under the symbols of tombs, weeping willow trees, and mournful female figures leaning on wreathed urns. The bleeding-heart was a favorite floral motive, lending itself gracefully both to the needle and to the subject. The enterprising Liverpool china-maker who dealt in subjects calculated to sell well in America sent over a shipment of cups and bowls decorated with a bust of Washington and a monument, with the motto, "Washington in glory, America in tears." A perfect flood of similar subjects in embroidery helped out with paint was turned out and they are still numerous.

From now on, in fact, the fanciful eastern flora gave way to real flowers, and as this was the dawn of America's sentimental period with its language of flowers, the designs began to show some botanical accuracy, and their attributes used with veiled meanings equal to the old Stuart times, though on a lower plane. Thus in the "Flower Vase, or the Language of Flowers and their Poetic Sentiments," the Columbine meant "I cannot give thee up," the Lily of the Valley conveyed the message "A Heart withering in secret," and the Ivy, "I have found one true heart."

We have a rather stately picture of life in the nation's capital during and after the administration of Washington. The President himself wore formal dress, and at Mrs. Washington's evening levees costumes were very elaborate and even magnificent. The effect of splendor was enhanced by the fact that men as well as women wore rich materials and variety of colors, along with their silver knee-buckles and shoe-buckles, lace cravats, swords and gloves. The Duke de la Rochefoucauld observes, in his account of his American travels, "I have seen balls on the President's birthday where the splendor of the room, the variety and the richness of the dresses, did not suffer by comparison with Europe."

New England, however, plodded along in its simple, humdrum way. John Fiske thus describes everyday life there at about the same time:

The occupations of the people were simple. There were few manufactures. . . . People seldom undertook long journeys, and mails were not very regular. It took a week to go from Boston to New York in a stagecoach, and all large rivers, such as the Connecticut, had to be crossed in boats, as none of them had bridges. In Boston, for example, the streets were unpaved, and the sidewalks unflagged. The better houses were usually built of brick, with little flower gardens in front, or lawns dotted with shrubbery. The furniture, silver and china in them were mostly imported from England, but some fine pieces of furniture were made at Dedham near by.

The people in New England's quiet homes were growing to be true intellectuals: a circle of cultured, well-read people living in small towns with good schools, college-bred ministers and teachers, and probably a printing press. We of today, with our wealth of illustrated magazines, public libraries, lectures and opportunities for travel, can scarcely conceive of life in a town like Northampton, Massachusetts, for instance, in 1825. The few periodicals which were published were eagerly awaited, passed from hand to hand and read from cover to cover. "Commonplace Books," which might be called homemade magazines, were kept; long passages from reading were copied and later discussed. Recipes, home remedies, embroidery patterns gleaned from every available source were collected and passed around. In my possession are three samplers all made within five years of each other in neighboring Massachusetts towns, Cummington, Chesterfield and Ashfield, with identical motives, showing how patterns or sources were shared among neighbors. Poems were written to celebrate every occasion, public and private. Albums and Treasuries and

Young Ladies' Garlands, almanacks and every kind of homemade production were the repositories of all manner of household wisdom and elegant fancy. Penmanship was considered an art, and most towns had a writing master who guided the infant hand, wrote calling-cards with elegant flourishes, and built up his copperplate script into ornamental achievements to decorate memorials and testimonials. The hand that guides a pen is usually at home with a pencil, and we see more than a little influence of these flourishes in designs. The sterner sex was often called upon for aid in drafting; in a petticoat border owned by the Exeter Historical Society, Mary Gilman of Gilmanton, New Hampshire, who worked it, generously gave her brother the credit for the strong, decisive lines of her blue-and-white flowers, dated 1795.

Crewel work survived for years into the new century, but it bears the marks of a survival, with a composite look to its details and no distinct personality, and it was increasingly carelessly done. The floral designs were used chiefly to decorate bonnet-strings, silk aprons, small bags and other feminine accessories. The custom of dressing beds with canopies, tester and curtains was going out.

Characteristic of these years is the scattered leaf design, suggested by the India muslins which were embroidered with small scattered sprigs and leaves, and popular too, no doubt, because large areas of fabric could be decorated more quickly and easily by spaced designs. All the crafts show the leaf motive, and it became common in printed cottons and dress goods as well. The makers of rugs could bring in actual leaves, lay them down and trace around them to plan a pattern, just as the stencil cutters drew delicate foliated shapes to decorate walls, chairs and trays. The maple, birch, maidenhair, lilac, bleeding-heart and strawberry leaves are all recognizable for different effects, sometimes separately, sometimes in repeat, very often in a triple spray. The cottage china made in England and used commonly in this country was decorated with similar sprigs and small leaves in delightful colors and often quite true to nature.

As patterns grew more slight and more geometrically planned, the older free-hand style began to disappear, and before long the art of needlework as a free expression was doomed. Designs were more and more copied from the latest suggestions in the household magazines of the day, like *Peterson's* and *Godey's* which vied with each other just as their successors do nowadays to produce something new and intriguing. Even "sketches" were copied from books of model trees, stone walls and nondescript buildings; some artistic souls had followed Mr. Adam's enthusiastic lead so closely and so literally that they went a step further than he and made artificial "ruins." A ruined temple lent an interesting air of melancholy to a garden, and similar depressing subjects are common in sketch books of the period.

The rise of cotton as a staple product, which had begun with Whitney's invention of the cotton gin during Washington's administration, was to revolutionize the whole textile industry. After this cotton grew to immense importance economically, and fabrics became so cheap that there was little use in continuing the laborious home production of thread. Printed goods had color and pattern, satisfying the feminine urge for decoration, and thus had a distracting influence on the needleworkers, and women were quite content with ready-made pieces by the yard.

We have dwelt before on the long preparation through many stages which is necessary in the growth and processing of thread and the production of homespuns and their decoration, and we can understand how precious the least scrap of cloth was to its maker, and how well founded was her pride in her achievement. In those early days when money was scarce, tangible possessions had solid worth and importance; shelves of piled snowy linen and soft blankets were an investment, and a bride who brought such a store to her husband made a real contribution to his estate. Now, wealth is to be reckoned rather in bank books and columns of figures—the wherewithal to buy a product in the making of which we have had no hand at all.

This marks the end of needlework as a spontaneous national art. While we had the homespun thread, which calls for an intimate and subtle coordination between foot, hand and turning spindle, we had an intimate personal product, taking into its formation something sensitive from the spirit and mood of the creator. When spindles are multiplied and driven by mechanical power, that triple fellowship is broken. The spinner no longer puts forth energy to use a tool with the hand, but controls the drive of a machine, and something entirely different is the result. Only spinners and weavers themselves can understand this to the full. And with the breaking off of the thread, we surrendered that fellowship, and the love of wrought decoration which was bound up with the fabric loosened and fell away.

VI

THE DEERFIELD REVIVAL

✿✿✿

THE last seventy-five years have contributed almost nothing, nationally speaking, to American needlework. If we are to characterize the work done during that time, we can only call it imitative. The reasons are not far to seek: loss of touch with the fabric-structure itself, owing to the prevalence of the machine; the opening of American markets to products from all over the world and the competitive urge to possess something new; and our own greatly enlarged opportunities for travel.

The sentimental period came to a somewhat gruesome climax with the use of human hair, not only in wreaths of dismal flowers and ringlets in the backs of large gold "breast-pins," but even in needlework, when long brunette strands were worked into minute initials and mottoes. "Fancy-work" was very much to the fore; shells, acorns, braid, beads, straw-flowers and worsted yarn all contributed their quota to the most fantastic creations. Perhaps it was the profusion of materials that went to the needleworkers' heads, for it seems as if our immediate ancestresses, so capable and practical in most things, did not use their common sense in this. Materials were assembled which were never born for each other. Lambrequins, made of cotton bed-ticking sewed in alternating stripes with velvet, and the whole "cat-stitched" together, are simply not sensible; and felt embroidered with spiders' webs and cat-tails in chenille is—beauty aside—a catcher of moths and dust, offset by no redeeming feature. Much as we revere Great-Aunt Emeline's memory, we cannot admire her crazy-quilt of silk and velvet pieces, its plan of construction suggesting the splintered points left by a stone in its passage through a window; pattern it cannot be called, for in a pattern the lines must bear some ordered relation to each other.

We have passed successively through the Berlin woolwork period with its slippers decorated with red and purple flowers, and cross-stitched hairy dogs carrying their master's cane in their jaws worked upon "catch-alls," the Biedermayer and Battenburg period, Mexican drawn-work, Swedish hardanger and hedebo, Italian cutwork, French eyelets and satin-stitch; we have decorated our intimate garments with Hamburg and tatting, crochet lace in wool for winter flannel petticoats and in cotton for summer nainsook ones, and the final enormity of "lazy-daisy," all of which left us poorer in design and more careless in execution than before.

But it is always darkest just before the dawn, and after the revolt in England against ugliness led by William Morris and his mediævalist brotherhood, and the lasting impress which he made on English taste by means of his printing press and tapestry works, a new spirit began to be reflected in America as well, which slowly but surely raised the standard of decoration and brought back sanity.

There have been many exponents of fine handicraft in this country working in many materials, through whom the new spirit began to spread. The Boston Society of Arts and Crafts was a pioneer, founded in 1897. Ten years later the National League of Handicraft Societies was organized, with constituent societies in many states; and in the interests of this movement a little magazine called *Handicraft* was published in Montague, Massachusetts, with Carl Purington Rollins as editor. Individual members of these groups began to experiment with the old designs and methods and the New England type of crewel work was more than once the subject of study for a special exhibition or project by the Boston Society and the Aquidneck Cottage Industries, for example; but for the most part their designs were their own in the new manner.

The founding of the Society of Blue and White Needlework in Deerfield, Massachusetts, in 1896, however, was an important event for the cause of needlework, because it dedicated itself to the study and revival of a truly American type and gave expression to a new enthusiasm. To borrow a phrase from Lewis Mumford, it was "the outcome of a warm, loving and above all intelligent commerce with the past." Not only did the work of this Society reach a high degree of excellence during its nearly thirty years of existence (it came to an end in 1925) but it stepped in just when the knowledge of this type of embroidery practised in the early days and the recognition of its value were on the point of disappearing, and thereby saved many things which might have been irrevocably lost. Also, it went the whole way and learned how to produce its own materials. Even today, the work of the Deerfield needleworkers is remembered and treasured, and its end is mourned, for it rekindled a flame of interest that has never quite gone out.

The founders were Miss Margaret C. Whiting and Miss Ellen Miller, both descendants of Colonial families, though not natives of Deerfield. They went there to paint the quaint old village, and from the friendship and artistic fellowship which sprang up between them, the little town was destined to receive a new lease of life; like so many small New England villages it had been left behind and forgotten by the swift race of modern life and many of its fine old houses were occupied by a few women left alone.

Both had modern training in design and they quickly saw the perfect setting of the place for a revival of the fine old country arts as a means of livelihood for some of these hard-pressed village people. They studied the existing examples of needlework preserved in ancient chests and in the private collections of the old Connecticut valley families; they were at once struck with the marked Oriental, and especially Persian characteristics of the designs, and delved into libraries and museums, studied stitches which were new to them, and began to build their structure. Their new designs were based upon the traditional ones, and exclusive possession of them was assured and protected by a trade-mark, a "D" in the center of a spinning wheel, which appeared on every piece of needlework done by members of the Society. They employed, at the height of activity, between twenty and thirty women of the village, carefully training them in stitches and insisting on fine workmanship, superintending every step of the way.

It was apparent from the first—as we have tried to prove in the foregoing pages—that this type of work with its close affinity to nature and its simplicity of feeling called for handmade linen. The commercial linens obtainable, with their over-bleached appearance and machine texture, were simply out of the picture. Those were years before the general popular interest in handicrafts had awakened and it was hard to find suitable handmade fabric, short of buying expensive imported pieces. In order to carry out the spirit of the old designs, they purchased homespun linens from Berea College and from weavers in Vermont and Georgia who had made a beginning at this craft, until they could start a weaving industry of their own. Proper shades of thread too were hard to find; machine-spun and chemically dyed threads were so artificial in appearance on the heavy linen that they were impossible. So the Society established a spinning and dyeing industry of its own, and was soon producing threads in nature-colors in three or four shades of blue, which gave the work its distinctive character and name. Later other simple colors were added, greens, madder, fustic and others.

In spite of myself, this account of the Deerfield Society's work must assume the character of a personal reminiscence, because its special appeal cannot be fully realized unless one has as a background a small picture of the Deerfield of those days. From the antiquarian's point of view the whole village was perfect: not an imitation or a studied reproduction of the past, but a living survival, completely unself-conscious. And what a past it was! Deerfield, along with Hadley, Hatfield and Sunderland, was one of the very early settlements in the Connecticut valley and had borne the brunt of the French and Indian wars. It went through a veritable martyrdom in 1675, and barely survived the second brutal massacre in 1704. For years there had been rivalry over this coveted strip of fertile river land, and these villages were settled by English pioneers who came from the Massachusetts Bay colony along what is still known as the Bay Path. They were a brave handful of men and women who ventured into the dreaded King Philip's country.

As a child living in a neighboring town, I was brought up on tales of Old Deerfield, fed on the stories written for children by Mary P. Wells Smith about the "Young Puritans." It was not difficult, on our visits to the old village with its hoary gray houses and the many memorial stones marking the spots where people had been surprised and slain or taken captive, to imagine an Indian lurking behind every tree. A visit to the museum in Memorial Hall was a fearful joy, as we gazed somewhat shrinkingly at the door with the hole gashed in it by a tomahawk through which a musket could be levelled by the Indian foe, and the pathetic little worn shoe lost by one of the child captives, which made the past very real to us. Bloody Brook still runs in its ancient channel, and there are many things unchanged which a childish imagination can seize upon in order to re-create those days of violence, fear and bloodshed. Perhaps the most poignant experience of all is a visit to the sunny, silent old grave-yard, now bird-haunted and peaceful, where so many of those brave hearts rest, and where rises the mound with its simple inscription, "The Dead of 1704."

The houses on either side of the wide, elm-shaded street have hardly changed since very early days. Many have never been painted, and time and weather have changed their texture to a soft gray velvet; small-paned windows and huge chimneys, sagging thresholds and loops of ancient grapevines make a convincing setting for the shadowy actors in those long-ago dramas, whose figures we could almost see walking along the paths which are humped with the gigantic roots of the old trees.

Every year in the height of the summer season, the Deerfield Society had an exhibition and sale, and throngs of tourists and customers arrived by the electric car or train, bicycle or horse-drawn vehicle. Doors stood open giving fascinating glimpses into narrow little halls with the patterns of very old wallpapers still to be seen, and steep narrow flights of stairs. I remember seeing four women sitting in hollow-square formation under the trees on a lawn in the hot summer afternoon, each at work on a corner of a large linen bedcover in blue and white needlework. They must have reached a high degree of skill to be able to merge their work on one piece so that no variation from the different hands would be noticed in the finished production.

Each house had a sign to indicate the nature of the work carried on within. There was the pine-needle basket house, and another where beautifully patterned raffia baskets were made; the house where the netting worker would spread out her lacy "canopy-tops" for beds, with their thousands of knots and deep fringe; the rug maker, and the worker who drew knotted patterns into white linen, and the Miss Allens who took wonderful photographs. But our favorite, the magnet among them all, was the large square house before which the sign of the Spinning Wheel hung, denoting the headquarters of the Blue and White Society. Brought up by my mother to love the needle and all its works, I was spellbound by the graceful designs and the soft colors with their little variations in tint between green and blue, and the general air of artistic competence in a kind of work so utterly different from that practised by the ordinary maker of "fancy-work" of those years.

A fine old bed would be dressed with a complete set of coverlet, curtains and valance done in shades of indigo on homespun linen. The walls would be hung with the larger pieces, squares and runners of various sizes, and even curtains with variations on the theme of the Tree of Life, beautifully drawn and blossoming in soft colors; the designs were quite in the spirit of the past but better drawn, and with subtly used stitches and colors beautifully blended. No one would ever take them for mere copies of old pieces; they had a personality and assurance all their own. As all the designs came from the same hands, the work developed a very individual and characteristic feeling. Often the basic lines of the designs were the same, with a variation in the flowers and other forms introduced, changed about and played upon like the notes in a piece of music. Little strawberries and thistles, clovers, birds, bees and berries were wrought into the borders, rivalling the illuminated pages in old books.

Tablecloths were being replaced on fashionable tables by round doilies, the predecessors of the present oblong place-mats, and the Society made a specialty of these doilies in different sizes. I set out at an early age to buy a whole dozen of each size, one at a time, for the price seemed exorbitant to my modest allowance. When I was married, several pieces of Deerfield work were among my wedding presents, and they are as sturdy and bright today as they were then, in spite of the years of use. Although the motive and border designs were adapted from the old crewelwork in wool, linen thread was used almost entirely. It is more practical and durable, not having such attraction for moths, and better withstanding the ravages of the laundry. This is why I can still furnish a few for photographing, these thirty years after.

The prices were high, but it was explained by the directors that every piece was as perfect as possible, and although such work was a luxury, full value was given. An embroiderer of the Society in its early days remembers how every stitch on a large coverlet so carefully embroidered was laboriously taken out after the discovery had been made that the color of the thread was not absolutely fast. Better that weary job beforehand, she said, than to have the imperfection discovered after the first washing and the whole piece ruined. This was the spirit which animated the Deerfield Industries. The Society was often asked to exhibit, but rarely had to submit to juries, for the master quality of its craftsmanship was easily recognized. A silver medal was awarded for color and design to the two founders by the Pan-Pacific Exposition to which they were invited to send a collection of Deerfield pieces.

In 1925, the Society of Blue and White Needlework came to an end. The World War made a break in that industry as in so many other things; it was impossible for some time to get good linens or find the necessary labor to produce good colors from the natural dyes, and what was more disastrous, there were no young people coming along who were interested at that time to learn the craft and lend their good young eyes and a degree of enthusiasm to it. After the death of Miss Miller, Miss Whiting wisely decided that a definite break-off was better than a gradual dwindling, and so the Society disbanded and the sign of the Spinning Wheel was called in. Examples of the early excellent vintage still in existence will increase in value with time, and the Deerfield workers are already becoming a tradition, a perfect little chapter bound up with the history of their lovely old village.

Deerfield today is again awake, for it is the site of three flourishing schools. Its old houses are in better repair than ever and its streets are full of young figures. The peaceful interlude of years with the women putting bright stitches of indigo, saffron, and rose madder into homespun linen under the trees will probably never return. But the Society did its bit to tide the village over a difficult time, from one phase of life to another. More than that, it rediscovered and handed on to us a fine art, having proved its lasting worth and beauty, and served as the link to insure the continuity of our needlework history.

This chapter may well end with a question. We have seen in the last few years a reawakening of interest all over the country in our past, its customs and costumes, its old dances, arts and humors. People are learning to raise herbs all over again, and studying the old cookery books; fine illustrated books and magazines are presenting every phase of the American scene. Every summer sees pilgrims from the western states driving along New England roads with guidebooks and cameras. The latest expression of this awakening is the American Index of Design which represents a great amount of research and study into our native arts and handicrafts, and the country-wide interest in New Hampshire's experiment in reviving the handmade methods and employing native materials in its League of Arts and Crafts. Perhaps we are learning that "the machine is a useful servant but a poor master," and that things made with the hands have a peculiarly satisfying quality which cannot be achieved by any other means.

Our present-day life is of such a profoundly different texture that it is impossible to enumerate the steps by which we have arrived at it. Perhaps the briefest way to describe what has happened to our homes is to say that a great science of "interior decoration" has grown up, stimulated and fostered by advertisement and skilful salesmanship addressed chiefly to women, who do most of the spending. Consequently the decoration of our homes has become feminine. We change its fashions just as we change the mode of our clothes, every year; we have no contemporary style, no definite school or order, partly perhaps because modern architecture is still in a state of flux, groping through the maze of new materials and their capacities for use. A house is a series of tableaux or episodes, each room a picture complete in itself, and taking on almost nothing from the origins and tastes of its occupant. We feel positively weighed down by the care of possessions, and escape the responsibility by disposing of them and transplanting our lives into the very shallow soil of a surface-life in a flat. But the dweller in a city can never be wholly independent; he must look to some one else for his food, his milk, his fuel, because he can produce none of these things himself.

How can we get back on solid ground again, and begin to produce something which shall be logically and soundly American? We must first of all establish in our own minds just what we wish to do. If we want to cut ourselves off from the past entirely and surround ourselves with an ultramodern setting, needlework and homespun is not for us at all. For that will be a machine-made place with a *decor* of shining surfaces in which handwork has no logical place, a product of America's growing-pains, continually changing.

But if we live in a home which is not merely of today but which holds continuity with a former time, if we are still proud of old mahogany and pine, the whole place hangs together, like the bits of color leaded into the pattern of a stained-glass window. All the arts contribute— china, glass, textiles, fine woods, silver, in color and line to make a friendly whole, with a final personal impress upon it like a signature.

There is no use in dreaming of the past, for it can never return, any more than the Time-stream can turn back and flow uphill. To try to copy the laborious methods of our ancestors, born of their limitations, would be but a foolish affectation. And yet there is something out of the past which is a truly native quality, inbred in our people, and therefore belonging to us like an heirloom. That is the true democracy and freedom of our home soil, which gives us our living.

The men and women who still live on the farms, therefore, are the hope of America for a normal, stabilized life; we have seen it before, and it is as true today. They realize the new economic conditions, controlled and manipulated by some far-away stock exchange or group of politicians, without being able to change or better them. But they are not ready to scrap everything belonging to the older times. As for their own daily lives on the home acres, dawn and moon and dark still go on. They get their weather reports and their political speeches over the radio now, instead of waiting for the stage to bring the daily paper; but they still retain their own views of the one by the set of the weather vane on their own barn or the cloud down over their particular mountain; and they still meditate upon the other with slow appraisal, making up their own minds in the end. There must be others, too, like-minded from inheritance and natural inclination, who look below the surface and think about these things.

So if our native arts and crafts are to survive and fill a place, it is not to the city people that we must look. It is to the sound sense and loyalty and the deep affection of our country people for what America has always stood for, and to what her three centuries of existence have given expression. And above all, these crafts must grow out of a need—the fundamental need which is born in a man to make something with his hands.

Here is an art, basically simple, bound up with our homes and our families. Our great-grandmothers sewed a record of events, large and small, into their homespun history. They saw life in a pattern, a picture. Have we less imagination and sensitive feeling than they? Perhaps modern life moves too fast and is on too vast a scale for us to attempt in carrying on the record. But we have the same human relationships, the same hills and sky, and always nature remains—the little flowers and animals and birds which we love, and the change of the seasons, to give us themes. Whether we record a transatlantic flight or some national centenary in our needleworked story or not, there is the ending of winter every year and the robin outside our window, and our own personal answer to the question as to what the things are which really matter.

Is it not about time to be picking up the threads again?

VII

NEEDLE IN HAND

✻✻✻

Fɪʀsᴛ, as the old recipe books have it, take your linen. If you are not a weaver, familiar with the over-and-under of the shuttle, perhaps you have never thought about its structure; and it is important that we should be familiar with the materials with which we are working because they govern our technique very definitely. A good exercise to familiarize oneself with the feel of the fabric is to draw out a thread across a small trial piece, and then run one in with a needle in its place, observing how the upper thread is loose and the under tight, and therefore picking up the tight one each time with the needle so as to hold the loose one firmly down. A round-thread linen of even texture will give a very nearly square mesh, so that a cross-stitch taken over two threads each way will make a perfect square, not tall and narrow as would be the case if the warp threads were coarser than the weft. A little practice with some of the simple counted-thread stitches on a sampler or small scraps of linen will soon give this feeling until you come to think of the fabric in squares like those on printed graph paper—the underlying structure of all woven fabrics.

These samplers are often useful for reference and for experimenting with problems of expression. No great artist ever painted a picture without preliminary trials and sketches. And needlework, like every art, has its rules and conventions, and the limitations of its materials. Having once accepted them we are free to use our own inventiveness and skill as we like to express our original thought. The lines which confine our design may be invisible ones, but they should be none the less real and definite; after getting them established, the less we think of their presence the more effortless will seem the result—which is the mark of the true craftsman. It is the unconscious eye which follows along the line and finds its pattern and rhythm agreeable.

Just as in the world of human contacts, that elusive thing we call etiquette is largely a matter of restraint and self-control, so there should be restraint in art; for what we call Pattern is really Discipline. We cannot take something direct from nature and transfer it to the fabric with all its little imperfections and variations; we must straighten it, even up the reverse side, bend it into a graceful line, or else we have no design. The leaf from which we worked may have been uneven; but if we make a row of crooked leaves, the spectator who views the finished piece and who does not see what we saw will be teased and worried by what seems to him a weak piece of drawing.

Decorative needlework which tries to reproduce nature exactly, in every shade and detail, is trespassing on another art, that of painting. If we try to make our decorative forms appear round by stuffing them up, and putting in their shadows, we are trespassing again on the art of sculpture. The etiquette of a good workman in textiles, therefore, demands that he should take his subject from nature, flatten it out and restrain it within seen or unseen lines, so that the finished decoration is one with its underlying material.

No such restraint is put upon the painter. His tool is a brushful of paint, which can lay down a broad stroke covering quite a little area at once; and as his paint is fluid he can run strokes together and merge his colors to get a natural effect. His intention is different, too; for he is painting a picture of something, whereas the needleworker is adapting something, picking out its characteristics and interpreting them on the cloth. The sculptor who chisels away the stone from which a figure emerges, and the potter who does the opposite by building up with pressure a soft material into a shape, must each work inside his rules; the wood carver who must consider the shape of his wood and the pull of its grain can take time going over and over his finish until he has reduced it to something which gives pleasure to the hand as well as to the eye and in which he has brought out the full beauty of the material; whereas the ironworker who must work quickly with a material of great strength and resistance while it is malleable has the opposite condition to contend with. All have problems set them by the nature of their materials.

The limitation of the needle requires that the unit should be one stitch, more akin to the line drawn with the pen than with the brush. It is the multitude of these small stitches carefully laid one by one that puts our design upon the fabric and makes it merge into its background. Oriental embroiderers who pass years of apprenticeship learning the art of "needle-painting," whereby they imitate the tints and shadows of flowers realistically or reproduce a landscape upon a screen with photographic faithfulness, have exhibited incredible skill and the result is needlework indeed, but with no suggestion of the textile underneath; they have set aside the rules which should govern the decoration of textiles, and the result is noteworthy only because they have done it so wonderfully. A piece of needlework should never be mistaken for anything else.

To be really good, our work must pass certain other tests. One of them is attractiveness to the eye, another is usefulness; and in both of these, simplicity is a great factor. The decoration of a thing should not interfere with its function, otherwise it becomes just another useless bit of "fancy-work." This need not be developed farther here, because I believe the public taste has advanced in this regard and that we do not have so many useless objects in our houses as there were a generation ago.

In making a design the first thing to do is to lay down its basic lines. From them and around them our decoration should grow. If the accessories or nonessentials become overelaborate, the line and its meaning become obscured and the result is fussiness and weakness. We must look at a good thing which we like and decide *why* we like it; in nine cases out of ten, the eye decides before the mind, picking out the vital lines and perceiving the plan. Like the vista in a garden, a path should lead somewhere to a point of interest; the eye unconsciously follows through to something beyond.

This must not be taken to mean that we must be able to draw a design freehand with masterly strokes before we can begin. We are not drawing an actual picture of an object, but indicating its characteristics; a wavy stem-line is far from being a real vine, though it has the characteristics of one in the pliable stem which can be drawn out into a border. The sheep which graze under the shade of a giant strawberry are not real sheep, and it is certainly not a real strawberry; but perhaps they make us think of something pleasant which is real in our memory. And when in difficulty with a motive for our work we can always do as our ancestresses did and make a simple arrangement of lines, building them up with ornamental stitches and getting our interesting effect in that way. Many times it is simplicity and an unfaltering line which give a piece its distinction. And so in making a design we must be ready to eliminate. There is a parallel here between our flowering sprays and the real ones used in the careful "arrangements" at flower shows. Some of the leaves produced by the natural growth must be nipped off to reduce the crowded impression and in order not to hide the basic line. And so, if you feel uncertain about your undecorated spaces and hesitate over adding a few more leaves and tendrils—Don't. Your doubt will usually have arisen from the right instinct.

Short Cuts.—So many of the typical examples of old New England work were decorated with floral forms that we almost take them for granted, and when we come to analyze them we find that they were planned roughly inside a circle, oval, or triangular shape. The stems were often a simple curved line, or a reverse curve like a letter S, or a triple spray. Sometimes they grew outward from a circle like a garland; but almost always their basic lines were simple. It was very often the prac- tice—coming down from Queen Anne's day—to bind the edge with a fold of homespun in a contrasting color, say blue, or put a twilled linen tape around it, and inside this to make a geometric border of some kind, such as a row of little half-circles, perhaps drawn around a spool, with their sides just touching, springing from this straight framing-line. Some- times the half-circles were built up in pyramids of three-two-one, with points inward toward the center.

I was once shown a bedquilt beautifully quilted all over in this scallop pattern, each row springing from the tops of the preceding row; and the tradition in the family was that this scallop was drawn around the end of an oval pewter platter. "And I've got the platter, too!" said the owner proudly. Now any one in drawing a half-circle or an arc can use a compass, or tie a string to the pencil and swing it around; but the fact that a pewter platter was requisitioned seems to add a little flavor. And it may be more natural for a woman not of a mechanical turn to think of choosing from the china shelf a cup, saucer, small plate or large one. In the descending scale, there is always a bottle, a large spool or a thimble. It is a real time-saver to cut out cardboard circles and ovals of different sizes and keep them for planning patterns; and also most convenient to cut out a length of wavy edge for stem-lines, perhaps one in small size and another in large shallow waves. This is very simple:

Rule a line, mark it off in one, two, or more inches, and then take some circular object and draw around its curve, first on one side of the line and then on the other, between the measured marks. Carry this around one corner too, and then in drawing a wavy vine pattern or border line, all the corners will measure alike. Measuring is very important; not only a ruler but a little six-inch rule should be one's constant companion. If nothing better is at hand, measure off the inches by quarters along the edge of an envelope and it will last for some time in your workbasket. These things sound too simple to mention, and yet few people think to equip themselves in this way before starting a piece of work, and it is the little things which are important in needlework.

A practice much to be commended is to hem the edge of your piece neatly before starting any decoration at all. One knows then just how large the area is to be, how wide the hem is, and how far inside it the work should be placed. Personally, I like some sort of a narrow decorated line, or at least a plain line of color around the hem-line. It acts as the frame around a picture and gives a finished look, as well as strength, especially if the decoration is not in the form of a border but in scattered motives.

Folding is also a very good way of insuring evenness in getting the design on; if there is some sort of a diagonally placed figure in a corner, it is easy to make a diagonal fold and lay the stem-line of the spray upon it, being sure that the most outside edges of the motive measure the same distance from the edge on both sides. In the case of a large piece like a tablecloth or a bedcover, it can be divided into quarters with a long running-thread in color, from which one can measure one's distances, and which can be easily pulled out when it is finished. If there are to be scattered motives over the surface, it is well to lay the piece out on a bed and do all the measuring at once with a tape measure, putting in a colored stitch at the very point where the center of the motives should come. There is no danger, if all the figuring is thus done before-hand, of getting one's work misplaced or off center.

Colors.—The type of work we are considering is best when it is com-paratively simple. As we have so often remarked, the early range of colors was limited; but as there was no attempt at naturalistic shading from light through many intermediate tones to dark, there was no neces-sity for the great color-scale we find on a modern color-card. Three shades were enough, dark, medium, and light, with the medium one predominating and the others used for contrast and emphasis. They were in the nature colors, blue, green, red or rose, brown, yellow or gold, and lastly violet. This color could be easily dispensed with, especially if the insipid shades of lavender are all one can get; the same can be said of pink; but we would add a deep tone of natural linen color which blends beautifully with the others and gives them added relationship with the linen background. The variations in the different lots of the old thread gave them delightful vagaries which were part of the blend although not by deliberate intent. We have no such limitations in our choice, but the fact remains that our results will be better if we use a simple scale. We are discussing a particular type of work; and a needle-woman inclined to more brilliant colors and more intricate effects will naturally choose some other style which will allow her more scope. For charm and distinction we believe there will never be anything more effective than blue alone, in its three or four shades.

Threads.—When crewel work was in its glory, it was done in the same thread, produced in the same manner, as the threads in the weaving, so that the finished work was an amalgam of related materials. If the linen was heavy and coarse, so was the embroidery thread; and on a fine piece like muslin or delicate linen, fine threads in smaller designs were used. Mrs. Burton Gates of Worcester, Mass., has an exquisite apron worked all in white on fine white linen with scattered sprays of flowers and leaves alternating with single oak-leaves and a few darned-in square motives. The style and stitch are characteristic of the good period, but on a miniature scale.

A medium heavy linen thread, equal in size to three strands of the six-strand D. M. C., is the best, or else the charming crewel wools which work up so softly when used in the overlaid stitch. Naturally it is only the exceptional person nowadays who is interested to spin and dye her own thread; this craft is being practised only by a few enthusiasts in the various Craft societies. The vast majority of workers buy their materials all prepared, and there are various brands of very good linen threads on the market, put up on cones or reels for the use of weavers. For a special piece of work it is always possible to buy white linen thread and have it dyed to the required shade. If the piece is something which will not require frequent washing, the crewel wools are most desirable, and one strand in the needle goes a long way.

Needle.—The best needle to carry the threads of suitable size is a so-called crewel or chenille needle, which has a large eye but a sharp point. The point enables you to place your stitch with precision, but the puncture made by the large eye brings your thread through without fraying or wearing it so that it lies smoothly. A too small eye will cause a lump where the thread doubles back and very soon a thin place is worn from the strain of pulling on it, which wastes a lot of thread in the end. This seems a very small matter, but many people do not consider the little things in time.

Stitches.—With colors limited to a few simple ones, more emphasis was put on stitches, in order to give interest. In Italy where very rich embroidery flourished and where silks were to be had in all sorts of fine shadings, the stitch would be very simple; whole areas were covered with Kensington-stitch or smooth satin-stitch, brilliantly shaded. But if one were to use great variety *both* in color and stitch on the same piece, the effect would be confused and restless. It is good training to do a piece of work occasionally all in white or one color, for the sake of building up one's stitch collection. There are only a few fundamental stitches: the plain laid stitches taken one at a time, the back-stitches, the loop-stitches, and the knot-stitches. All the elaborate ornamental effects are variations and combinations of these, or one stitch built upon another, as Pekinese-stitch, which is a loop built upon a line of back-stitch.

In many delightful old pieces it was often the habit to outline a petal or leaf simply, and then to fill it in with little counted-thread stitches in blocks or lines or seeded effects. Miss Whiting in Deerfield owns a wonderful fragment of a bed-valance exquisitely done in but two or three shades of blue but with an ingenious variety of these filling-stitches, which she considers a document of artistic importance and which has had a good deal of influence on the Deerfield ideas.

Stitches are a most important part of the worker's stock in trade. We might call them her alphabet, with which she can spell out the thought which is in her mind. To embroider a basket of flowers, for instance, she can employ one of the many filling-stitches built up on the threads of the linen which will reproduce the plaited texture of the basket. The stitch with which she works the leaves may indicate the central vein and the slant up to the point. The flowers can be given the appearance of radiating out from the center, with little knots for the heads of stamens; or, if they are in profile, a spring outward from the sheath or from the point of their stem. The connecting lines should be definite, so that this feeling of growth is expressed; the stem should meet the flower firmly, not leaving a break or a feeble, sketchy line, and the leaves should grow from the stems, not float loosely in air. There are stitches for putting in the little acorn cups, the bachelor's-button petals with their saw-tooth ends, for the special growth of thistles, pine-cones, ferny leaves. There are ways of making little wavy lines to suggest how water flows, the feathers in a bird's wing, and so on. The Chinese are adepts at this and their work well repays study—and this, surprisingly enough, brings us right around again to where our ancestors were. We are continually meeting the Oriental influence in unexpected places.

A friend in the country, displaying to me a rather primitive old piece of embroidery of a stiff little basket of prim flowers, commented: "It's got kind of a set look, hasn't it? But come to think of it, New England folks are kind of set themselves." Perhaps that, in a nutshell, is the secret of the charm of these old-time American pieces—the fact that under the fingers of those rather set and serious people, nature could blossom and the dull fabric break forth into soft gayety and color.

To end up with a New Englandism, we might do worse than to learn something of their way of surveying the New England scene, and perhaps in these few pages there may be the germ of a thought which will some day blossom out into blue again.

INDEX

INDEX

✿✿✿

Sunderland, Indian ravages at, 31, 70
Swan, design of the, 58; symbol of royalty in design, 18
Swedish hardanger, 67
Swedish hedebo, 67
Symbols, religious, in art, 18

Tablecloth, described, 42, 56
Tables, duck foot, 43
"Tag-locks," practice of weaving, 12
"Tape-stick," a, 37
Tapestries, pictured, concept of, 14
"Tapestry pictures"—the rage of the period of James I, 22
"Tapet," the, floor covering of the Queen Anne period, 21
Tatting, 67
Tea Leaf, pattern for bed-quilt, 47
Teaspoons, engraved, pattern of, 48
Tent-stitch, the, in early needlework, 14
Thistle, design of the, 18, 41, 58
Threads, 83, 84
Trade mark, the Deerfield, 69
"Treasuries," 62
Tree of Life, versions of the, in England, 15; design of the, 15, 16, 30, 40, 48, 72
Trinity, the trefoil of the, as a symbol, 18
Triple form design, the, 38
Triple spray, the, 43
Tritons, in design, 19
Tudor rose, the, design of, 26, 56

Tudor style, the heavy character of, in needlework, 14
Tudor times, influence of, on design, 15, 52
Tulip, the, design of, 30, 42, 48
Turkey-work, 21, 24

Unfinished piece, description and story of an, 59
Unicorns, in designs, 19
Universal stitch, the, 37

Valance, embroidered, described, 41
Vermeer, "Turkey work," shown in paintings of Dutch interiors by, 24
Vermont, weavers in, 69
Victoria and Albert Museum, fine coverelet exhibited at the, 28

Wallpapers, designs of, 34, 35, 48, 54; first appearance about 1735, of, 53; French, 58
"Wallets," 38
Warren, Mercy, quoted, 46
Washington, George, death of, 2, 61; and the pine-tree flag, 28; family, coat of arms, 46; bestowal of the Purple Heart by, 48; fine costumes of the time of, 61; shown in wallpaper of the day, 53
Washington, Martha, her use of the shell design, 39; thrifty practices of, 59; evening levees of, 61
"Wavy stem-line," English use of, 36

Wayside Inn, at Sudbury, 31
Weaving, pioneer, 30; necessity for, 44; of the Deerfield Society, 69
Webb, Miriam, 39
Westfield, settlements at, 31
Wethersfield, settlements at, 31
Whig Rose pattern, the, 26
Whiting, Miss Margaret C., a founder of the Deerfield Needlework Society, 68, 73, 85
Wigs, use of, 37
Winthrop, John, arrival of, 9; quoted, 30
Witchcraft and the cross as a symbol of protection, 40
Women, Colonial, their responsibility for the household clothing, 11
"Wood-workers" of New England shipyards, 55
Wool, scarcity of at Plymouth, 9; a prime Colonial need, 11; weaving of, 12
World War, fervor of the, 45; destructive influence of the, 73
Wright, Polly, of Hatfield, Mass., 43

York, Maine, needlework in (1745), 40
Yorkshire, weavers from, 30
Young Ladies' Garlands, 63
"Young Puritans," the, 70

Zulueta, Professor Francis de, historical research of, 20